D0860054

PROPHETIC
PREACHING

then and now

by

Roland Q. Leavell

BAKER BOOK HOUSE
Grand Rapids, Michigan
1963

PROPHETIC PREACHING: Then and Now

Library of Congress Catalog Card Number: 63-19098
Copyright 1963 by Baker Book House

Printed in the United States of America

PHOTOLITHOPRINTED BY CUSHING - MALLOY, INC.
ANN ARBOR, MICHIGAN, UNITED STATES OF AMERICA
1963

FOREWORD

"The bugle call to a heavenly warfare must be given with no uncertain sound" is a typical word from Dr. Roland Q. Leavell's *Prophetic Preaching, Then and Now*. There is a challenge to preachers in this book. It is stirring. It is both practical and lofty, both convicting and loving, both pungent and inspiring. All of us preachers need its message.

This book in its entirety is built upon The Word. The author exalts Jesus and Moses as the supreme examples of prophetic preachers. Out of the words of these great preachers and those who have followed in their train he builds messages that deal with preachers' problems frankly, unflinchingly, and evangelistically.

Dr. Leavell's remarkably rich and varied experience prepared him in a peculiar sense to speak to his fellow preachers as he does in this work. The lives of few men have embodied so much experience from the pastorate, the evangelistic ministry, the responsibilities of a denominational leader, the visions of a seminary president, the passion for teaching Biblical truth, and the arts of an author of books designed to aid preachers.

Dr. Leavell's determination to spend his energies and talents to the utmost in the prophetic ministry is repre-

8141

sented by this book. It was brought to a conclusion in the midst of many months of Bible teaching in the churches combined with continual preaching. Though in retirement because of his health, it was his joy to continue this kind of ministry. Two weeks before the Lord's call came to a ministry in heaven, he wrote at length to the author of this foreword to express his appreciation for suggestions concerning the text and to indicate his own efforts in bringing it to a completion.

To those who knew Dr. Leavell well and who loved him deeply this work will remain as his challenge to us to preach like the prophets.

J. Wash Watts
New Orleans Baptist Theological Seminary

INTRODUCTION

The importance of preaching cannot be exaggerated. God-called preachers must fulfill their sacred missions in the pulpit if the kingdom of God is to be advanced. In today's crisis-ridden world and in a nation where paganism is progressing with monstrous strides, the bugle call to a heavenly warfare must be given with no uncertain sound.

There is an ever-increasing displacement of God through the idolatry of money-worship and materialistic greed. The nation is suffering from secularism in education, from decay of home life and tragic divorces, from increase in delinquency and crime, from the fearful ravages of the age-old demon of alcoholic drinking, from the sordid sins of sensuality and sexual promiscuity, from mere formality or gross negligence of worship of God, from positive agnosticism or practical atheism.

There are no new sins; these sins have just changed their outer garments. No sins have passed away; all the distressing trends of today were prevalent in Old Testament times and denounced by the prophets. The antidote for these social and spiritual diseases is the same as it was then, namely, God's gospel preached by holy men under the direction of the Holy Spirit.

This study of Old Testament preaching has been impelled by a heart full of genuine love for young preachers and genuine prayer for their effectiveness through their sermons. God has matched their glorious powers with this challenging hour. False religions, distorted thinking, and corrupt living can be defeated only by sincere worship of the God of righteousness and truth, by earnest searching for direction in the infallible Word of God, and by the Spirit-guided proclaiming of the gospel of the Son of God.

The ideal of preaching like the Old Testament prophets can be attained very rarely, if ever at all. Shakespeare expressed it strikingly:

> "If to do were as easy as to know
> what were good to do, chapels had
> been churches, and poor men's
> cottages princes' palaces."
> —Merchant of Venice
> Act I, Scene ii

But every preacher can commune with God like a prophet, can build character like a prophet, can pray like a prophet, can abhor sin like a prophet, can love souls like a prophet, and can try under the Holy Spirit to preach like a prophet.

May heaven's choice blessings of wisdom, power and grace rest upon every preacher whose ideal is to scale the lofty heights of prophetic preaching.

Roland Q. Leavell

CONTENTS

"We have also a more sure word of prophecy; whereunto ye do well that ye take heed, as unto a light that shineth in a dark place, until the day dawn, and the day star arise in your hearts:

"Knowing this first, that no prophecy of the scripture is of any private interpretation.

"For the prophecy came not in old time by the will of man: but holy men of God spake as they were moved by the Holy Ghost."

—II Peter 1:19-21

CHAPTER ONE

PROPHETIC PREACHING

> "The Spirit of the Lord is upon me, because he hath anointed me to preach the gospel to the poor; he hath sent me to heal the broken-hearted, to preach deliverance to the captives, and recovering of sight to the blind, to set at liberty them that are bruised, to preach the acceptable year of the Lord."
>
> —Luke 4:18-19

The Lord Jesus Christ, the prophet of Galilee, is the divine pattern for all preachers. He was sent by the Heavenly Father to preach. He was anointed by the Holy Spirit to preach. Preaching was the chief method by which he implanted the truth of God into the minds and hearts of his believing followers. He lit his torch with fire from off the altar of heaven, and took the light into a benighted, sin-darkened world. The flaming words of truth which he preached attracted the attention of the multitudes, for fire is easily noticed in the darkness.

The sacred eloquence of the young prophet of Galilee attracted "great multitudes of people from Galilee, and from Decapolis, and from Jerusalem, and from Judaea, and from beyond Jordan" (Matthew 4:25). The multitudes flocked to hear him because he preached a sure word from God in heaven to hungry-hearted men on earth. He preached eternal truth, the glad news of the gospel.

Second only to Jesus, Moses was the tallest in the mountain range of the prophets, the most august character in antiquity. He brought vital messages directly from God to the people, messages about monotheistic theology, about morals, about social righteousness, about legal justice, about national policies and military strategy.

Moses' sermons in Deuteronomy form the text book from which so many prophets in the succeeding generations learned the rudiments of their mission and messages. This is especially true of the great prophets of the Eighth Century B.C.—Isaiah, Hosea, Amos and Micah. The Lord Jesus knew the writings of Moses intimately, quoted his sayings frequently, adhered to his teachings loyally, and fulfilled his prophecies gloriously.

Moses had the grandeur of Isaiah, the vision of Ezekiel, the passion for righteousness of Amos, the tender love of Hosea, the intense patriotism of Jeremiah, and the erudite mind of the Apostle Paul.

"And there arose not a prophet since in Israel like unto Moses, whom the Lord knew face to face."

—Deuteronomy 34:10

Clarion Call for Prophetic Preaching

There is a current and constant call for prophetic pulpit preaching. People have a genuine heart-hunger for the meat of the Word and the bread of life. A. T. Robertson, far-famed teacher of New Testament a generation ago, had a quaint way of sadly bemoaning the fact that the "poor hungry sheep look up to the food rack, and are not fed. All they hear is the wind whistling through."

Preachers are divinely called to preach, to preach in power and demonstration of the Spirit. Too many sermons are bland, innocuous, soporific. They deal in vague abstractions, pleasing platitudes, psychological theories, and watered-down theology, instead of telling people how to get the righteousness of God in their hearts through Christ. The water of life should not be handed out in half-pint cups.

When a prominent or desirable church pastorate becomes vacant, usually there are scores and perhaps hundreds of recommendations or personal applications for the place. However, a pulpit committee often takes months upon months searching for a man whom the church desires for pastor. Why do they search so long? They are looking for a man of God with a message from God, a man whose heart is ablaze with spiritual zeal to lead men to God. A congregation will overlook some other deficiencies and even some faults in a pastor if only he is a good preacher, with God's message. They want assurance from God that they have received the gift of salvation personally. They see a decaying society, and they want to hear the causes exposed, the remedy explained. Most churches are ready to call a man who has a soul burden, a heart passion and a prophetic urgency.

What Is Prophetic Preaching?

Prophetic preaching is preaching like the prophets. Preaching was one of the most unique and distinguishing characteristics of Jehovah worship during Old Testament times. Who can measure the influence of these holy men of old on their generations and throughout the centuries which have followed? "Thus saith the Lord" was their message, and preaching was their method of communicating it.

Preaching has been and still is pre-eminently vital to the spreading of the Christian faith. In order to build the kingdom of heaven, Jesus established the gospel as the essential message, the church as the promotional agency, and preaching as the principal means of persuasion. The early Christian fathers knew that Christ would save men's souls and that his gospel would save society from ignominy, despair, and decay. They preached that the kingdom of heaven was at hand. They predicted a new heaven and a new earth wherein righteousness would reign.

What is prophetic preaching? What is good preaching? Good preaching is a sermon that is preached with a good delivery, but much more. It means a well-prepared message with food for thought which is organized in proper homiletical form, but much more. Lack of some of these qualities can be forgiven if the preacher's soul is burdened with a message from God to men, and if his soul is ablaze with zeal to deliver it. His heart must be "pregnant with celestial fire" (Gray's *Elegy*).

One can learn something about the meaning of the term "prophetic preaching" from the original Old Testament word *nabhi,* translated prophet. Hebrew scholars say this word means a speaker, an announcer, a proclaimer, a herald. It is used nearly three hundred times in the Old Testament. A *nabhi,* a prophet of God, is a forth-teller. He is God's mouthpiece who delivers a message of God, when he is possessed with absolute certainty that it is divine truth coming directly from God, and when a heaven-born compulsion to deliver the message is upon him. When the inspiration for preaching is from God, it will be delivered authoritatively and with urgency. One preaches prophetically when he is under authority like Amos:

"Surely the Lord God will do nothing, but he revealeth his secret unto his servants the prophets.

Prophetic Preaching

> "The lion hath roared, who will not fear? The Lord God hath spoken, who can but prophesy?"
>
> —Amos 3:7-8

The preacher who merits being called a prophetic preacher must feel that he is under a spiritual compulsion like Paul when he said: "Necessity is laid upon me; yea, woe is me, if I preach not the gospel" (I Corinthians 9:16).

Prophetic preaching is not something merely thought out, or inferred, or hoped, or feared. It is directly inspired by the Spirit of God, an inspiration which gives power to a preacher's sermon preparation through study, meditation and prayer.

Some people think prophetic preaching always means foretelling future events. Frequently God used current conditions and events to open a prophet's vision to foresee results in the future. This is only a part of the meaning of the term, and not necessarily the major part. Old Testament prophets were not like almanac makers, predicting dates and events. They were forth-tellers more frequently than foretellers. They were truth-tellers, message-bearers, mouthpieces for God. Prophetic preaching dealt with the past and the present as well as the future. The Old Testament prophets were interpreters of history's lessons about moral and spiritual issues. They were "seers," men who knew the condition of their present world, in the light of which they praised or denounced or instructed people about their way of life. They had an understanding of the past and present when they "dipped into the future" to foretell the impending judgments of God.

The ideal is for a preacher to step forth like a herald with a personal message from the King of kings for each individual listener. It is said that once while Charles Haddon Spurgeon was preaching with impassioned earnestness a little girl in the vast audience asked with anxious concern, "Mother, is Mr. Spurgeon speaking to me?" Prophetic preaching did not inspire the phrases "dull as a sermon" and "prosaic as a parson." Jeremiah said God asked the question: "Is not my word like as a fire? saith the Lord; and like a hammer that breaketh a rock in pieces?" (Jeremiah 23:29).

Prophetic preaching does not just happen. It does not come automatically with a seminary degree, nor with ordination to the ministry, nor with a call to a pastorate. It is not by intellectual might nor by ecstatic emotion, but by the Spirit of God when he lays hold upon a preacher to deliver a life-and-death message to men. Sometimes prophetic preaching is abrupt, often it is explosive, frequently it is disturbing, but always it is moving and purifying and refreshing. It will not return void, but will accomplish God's purpose in the lives of men and nations (Isaiah 55:11).

The gospel should be communicated boldly, fearlessly, simply, earnestly, lovingly, "as from a dying man to dying men." There is no power in vague generalities, nor irrelevant theories, nor that which creates doubt in the minds of the hearers. People have doubts and theories enough; they are hungry-hearted for the truth from heaven. An ideal sermon is delivered in the language understood by the people, answers some problem of the people, and inspires a more godly life by the people. The poet beautifully describes the aims of a worthy preacher:

> "Unskilled he to fawn, or seek for power
> By doctrines fashioned to the varying hour:
> For other aims his heart had learned to prize,
> More bent to raise the wretched than to rise.
>
> "And, as a bird each fond endearment tries
> To tempt its new-fledged offspring to the skies,

Prophetic Preaching

He tried each art, reproved each dull delay,
Allured to brighter worlds, and led the way."
—Goldsmith, *The Deserted Village*

The content of prophetic preaching always is built around some profound doctrine which is pertinent to everyday life. Theology is the steel structure upon which every message is built. Not every preacher can preach a great sermon every time, but there is no excuse for preaching on a little and unimportant subject. There is no time for drivel when people are confused and frustrated and lost. May God deliver such people from clever entertainment, or mere reviewing current events, or "pink tea" dissertations on recent theories about psychology. Prophetic preaching is based on "Thus saith the Lord."

The prophets used apt illustrations and graphic metaphors in order to fix spiritual truth in the minds of the hearers. A well-built sermon is like a well-built house. It has doctrinal structure like steel, able discussion like well-built walls, and illuminating illustrations like clear windows. Jesus set the divine pattern in how to illustrate spiritual truths. Who could fail to understand what the Saviour was teaching when he gave such illustrations as that of the prodigal son, or the good Samaritan, or the rich farmer fool who died?

A number of the prophets even dramatized their illustrations in order to make them more effective. Jeremiah put a yoke about his neck while urging Judah to submit to Babylon (Jeremiah 27:2; 28:10). Ezekiel cut his hair and beard with a razor and divided it into three parts (Ezekiel 5:1-4). One part he burned, one part he smote with a knife, one part he scattered to the wind—illustrating how Judah would be treated. Isaiah walked the streets of Jerusalem barefooted and stripped of his outer garments, to declare dramatically how Assyria would lead the Egyptians as prisoners in shame (Isaiah 20:2-4).

It is entirely too frequent that people leave a preaching service, saying, "What in the world was the preacher driving at?" The people who hear Hosea or Jeremiah or John the Baptist most surely did not say that about the preaching they heard. The Old Testament prophets spoke in graphic language about things relevant to the daily living of their hearers, and made their sermons effective by pointed, personal application. For example, John the Baptist not only denounced sin and demanded repentance, but he told exactly what sins the people were committing and exactly how they should act to prove that they were repentant.

Permanence and Power of Prophetic Preaching

The throb of a true prophet's heart can be heard and felt throughout the ages to come. Truth can be hidden but it cannot be killed. Nothing can be an adequate substitute for prophetic preaching in advancing the kingdom of God. The printed page is a mighty instrument in propagating truth, but it cannot substitute for the flash of a speaker's eye, the sincerity in a prophet's voice, the pathos of a preacher's appeal, and a loving message which comes from the heart of a man of God. Pastoral ministries are useful and influential and quite necessary. Organization is effective and promotion can be dynamic. Sympathetic counseling is consoling and often vitally helpful. Rituals and ceremonies are pleasing and inspiring. But preaching, good preaching, God-inspired, Spirit-filled, and Christ-centered preaching, is God's supreme plan for building his kingdom.

Prophetic Preaching

"It pleased God by the foolishness of preaching to save them that believe."

—I Corinthians 1:21

Prophetic preaching has been an integral and vital part in every forward Christian movement or revival. Through the centuries God has touched the hearts of preachers with spiritual fire and made their tongues like spiritual flames. The ministry of gospel preaching is the pinnacle of the vocations of men. One should accept a call of God to preach with profound thanksgiving, heart-felt humility, and an all-compelling sense of responsibility.

FOR BIBLE STUDY AND DISCUSSION

1. How is the call of God to a preacher different from his call to a physician or teacher or business man?
2. Tell about the call of God to Moses, to Isaiah, to Jeremiah, to Ezekiel, to Amos, to Jonah, to Matthew, to Paul. Tell about their different difficulties about responding. Are preachers called like that today?
3. Discuss the pastors in the city, or the pastors of your church during the past twenty years, as to which one is most like an Old Testament prophet. Which of the prophets does he seem to be most like?
4. Study the life of Christ to see what emphasis he placed on preaching (Matthew 5-7, 10, 13, 24-25).
5. Discuss the different styles of delivery by the Old Testament prophets. Which one was most statesmanlike? the most rhetorical? the most emotional? the most patriotic? the most visionary? the sternest? the tenderest? the most Christlike? the most poetic? the most practical? the most encouraging?

CHAPTER TWO

PROBLEMS OF A PROPHET

> "Woe is me, my mother, that thou hast borne
> me a man of strife and a man of contention to
> the whole earth! I have neither lent money on
> usury, nor men have lent to me on usury; yet
> every one of them doth curse me."
> —Jeremiah 15:10

Bless Jeremiah's old heart! Many a prophet like him, since his time, has bemoaned the day that his mother gave him birth. Many a preacher has been discouraged like Elijah was when under the juniper tree, after some modern Jezebel has crooked her finger at him in criticism or threat:

> "But he himself went a day's journey into the wilderness, and came and sat down under a juniper tree; and he requested for himself that he might die; and said, It is enough; now, O Lord, take away my life; for I am not better than my fathers."
> —I Kings 19:4

In spite of the heartaches that a prophet will have and the bitter tears he is likely to shed, his message need not be in vain.

Men will listen to preaching when it is prophetic preaching. They will listen to a polished nobleman like Isaiah, if he has had a vision of the Lord and is sure that God has said, "Go, and tell this people" (Isaiah 6:1-9). People will hear eagerly a rustic like Micah, if he has a message from God about the way to live, a message such as Micah had:

> "He hath showed thee, O man, what is good: what doth the Lord require of thee, but to do justly, and to love mercy, and to walk humbly with thy God?"
>
> —Micah 6:8

Men will flock to hear the warning to "Prepare to meet thy God" (Amos 4:12), if the preacher is seething like Amos with a God-given indignation at the personal and social unrighteousness of the privileged people about him. Men will follow the leadership of a man, if he like Moses has learned the secret of victorious living during a mountain-top experience of communion with God. People will love a preacher, if he like Hosea is possessed with a heart-gripping emotion about the love of God. People will be eager to go hear a man like Isaiah who comforts and encourages and allures to the One by whose stripes men can be healed.

Perils of a Prophetic Preacher

No thinking man enters a preaching ministry for his own benefit. No one desires to be thought of as a fanatic, or troubler of Israel. Prophets are badly needed, but they are not universally wanted. The Lord Jesus said: "A prophet is not without honor, save in his own country, and in his own house" (Matthew 13:57). He wept over Jerusalem as he lamented, "O Jerusalem, Jerusalem, thou that killest the prophets, and stonest them which are sent unto thee" (Matthew 23:37).

The Apostle Paul did not encourage young men to enter the ministry as a place of ease and security. He exhorted Timothy to endure hardness as a good soldier of Jesus Christ (II Timothy 2:3), and Chapters 3 and 4 are given to details of the difficulties and opposition he must face. The recitation of Paul's perils, given in II Corinthians 11, would turn any young man away from the ministry except one who is conscious of a divine call.

The author of Hebrews, in the chapter that has been called the roll call of the prophets, wrote:

> "Others had trial of cruel mockings and scourgings, yea, moreover of bonds and imprisonment: they were stoned, they were sawn asunder, were tempted, were slain with the sword."
> —Hebrews 11:36-37

In spite of the sufferings of the prophets Jesus said:

> "Blessed are ye, when men shall revile you, and persecute you, and say all manner of evil against you falsely, for my sake. Rejoice, and be exceeding glad: for great is your reward in heaven: for so persecuted they the prophets which were before you."
> —Matthew 5:11-12

Prophets Must Be Models of Courage

Preaching about moral living and on controversial issues is always unpopular and sometimes perilous, when the people desire a way of life which is contrary to the righteousness of God. A prophet usually is criticized and often persecuted if he preaches social reformation, Christian attitudes toward minorities, reform in politics, sobriety regarding alcoholic beverages, and sanctity of the marriage vow. In Old Testament times the priests, false prophets, plutocrats, and even the royal families turned bitterly against the prophets who preached righteousness. Unholy people want to preserve the *status quo*.

Tradition says that Isaiah was sawn asunder. Jeremiah suffered untold vilification, bitter hatred, plots against his life, horrible imprisonment in a miry cellar, and abduction into Egypt to eke out his old age in exile. Amos was driven out from Israel by Amaziah the priest at Bethel. John the Baptist was imprisoned and then beheaded. The blessed Lord Jesus was nailed to a cross.

To preach prophetically necessitates that one live dangerously. It always requires conviction, character, and courage. One may be threatened like Peter, imprisoned like Paul, banished like Chrysostom, martyred like Savonarola, excommunicated like Luther, refused the use of pulpits like Wesley, asked to resign like Jonathan Edwards, banished like Roger Williams, or be the victim of jealousy like multiplied thousands of successful preachers. Through it all a modern preacher may well have statesmanship like Isaiah, courage to stand alone for right like Elijah, clarity of thought like Micah, longsuffering like Jeremiah, and love like Hosea.

Lincoln spoke like a prophet when he said, "I am not bound to succeed, but I am bound to be true." God does not promise a prophet success, much less popularity; God promises spiritual power. This much is certainly true: a preacher himself must wear the breastplate of righteousness when he reproves the faults of others, or else the one whom he is attacking will stick him under the fifth rib with a public revelation of the preacher's shortcomings. Only a right way of living can give a preacher the rightful privilege to preach righteousness to others.

Church Life Is Complex and Demanding

One of the perennial problems of a would-be modern prophet is the demand upon a preacher's time made by so many other things that he does not have time to prepare his sermons. It is unspeakably tragic for a preacher to "beat the air" before his congregation, unprepared in mind as well as heart for his prophetic mission of heralding some eternal truth from God.

Church life is growing more complex and more demanding all the while. The organizations demand time. Pastoral duties are pressing. Calls for counseling are clamorous. Denominational engagements are constant. Civic responsibilities are numerous. All these make disastrous inroads into a preacher's time for study, prayer, sermon preparation, and meditation.

A pastor of a moderate-sized church cannot do everything that some people expect of him. A preacher is expected to make more calls than a physician, settle more problems for people than a lawyer, and write more articles than the editor of a county newspaper. A pastor must be a better financier than a bank cashier, for people bring their money to the bank, but the pastor must raise the church budget through voluntary gifts. He must be a better organizer than a mill superintendent, for he must keep his organization intact with volunteer labor. He must be a better scholar than a teacher or professional lecturer, because they use their material over and over, but a preacher must deliver new sermons with fresh approaches to the same people week after week. A preacher must maintain better public relations than a congressman; a congressman can get elected by only 51 per cent of the votes, but a preacher must stay elected by virtually 100 per cent of the deacons and other members.

A pastor is called upon to perform both priestly and prophetic functions. Like a priest he must counsel, comfort, conduct funerals, perform wedding ceremonies, and visit people. Like a prophet he must commune with God, prepare sermons, and then herald zealously the good news about God's forgiving love and sustaining grace through

Christ. The multitude of priestly services should never be allowed to usurp the place of prophetic preaching. Preaching is the supreme task of a prophet; preaching should be given the supreme place in his ministry. The good should never be allowed to become an enemy to the best. It is pathetic when a preacher comes to church on Sunday morning unprepared to preach, fearfully uneasy and nervously ill-at-ease because he has to say something, rather than joyously excited because he has something to say.

Mature preaching comes from fervent prayer, arduous study of God's Word, and quiet meditation about every phase of the message. Many prophets of old developed their messages while they were in solitude with God: Moses on Sinai, Elijah at Cherith, Amos while tending the herds, Jeremiah in eschewing wedding feasts, Ezekiel in exile, John the Baptist in the wilderness of Judea, Paul in Arabia. While in quiet detachment a prophet may hear the "still small voice."

Prerequisites of a Prophet

The first prerequisite of a prophetic preacher is to feel that God has laid his hand upon him and thrust him out irrevocably into a preaching ministry. A pastor or organizer or promoter may be developed out of almost anyone who has abilities which he will dedicate in service. Such is not true of a prophet. Some enter a preaching ministry and flame up for a time like a torch, but the torch fire soon dies if it is not lit on the altar of heaven by God's eternal purpose. A prophetic ministry is not the place for occasional tourists.

Moses had such a life-changing and destiny-determining call in Horeb when he saw the burning bush. Isaiah had that experience while he was worshipping in the temple

(Isaiah 6:1-10). Jeremiah in Anathoth heard the call of God, saying that he was ordained of God to be a prophet unto the nations (Jeremiah 1:4-5). Without that conviction, he could never have endured all that he did. It was on a stormy day in Babylon that Ezekiel heard the voice of the Spirit expressly commissioning him to preach to the children of Israel (Ezekiel 1:4; 1:28—2:3). Throughout the records and writings of the prophets there are thrilling accounts of how God spoke to men and through them to the multitudes (Joel 1:12; Amos 7:15; Jonah 1:1-2).

Modern prophets well may emulate the traits of the prophets of old. These men of God had unimpeachable moral characters and unwavering courage. They were deeply pious, sincerely humble. They were unceasing in their prayer life. They had convictions about right and wrong, and were willing if necessary to die for the right. They displayed unflinching courage in the delivery of their messages from God, and were heroically brave under persecution.

The prophets were princely pulpiteers, a quality born of an intense sense of mission, deep convictions, heart-felt love and proper training. Some were eloquent; some were plain-spoken; some were fiery. Some prophets used words which pierced like a rapier; some thundered loudly into the hearer's ears; some sobbed out their broken-hearted appeals. They used visions, imagination and dreams. They drew upon the resources of history, literature, and poetry. Their sermons were made vivid with illustrations from nature and from everyday life. Every art of effective speaking was used—figures of speech, humor, sarcasm, emotion, teaching, controversy, evangelistic appeal.

The prophets were different each from the others and

individualistic, yet all of them spoke in the language of the average man. Any man on the street who heard could know what was on the prophet's heart. If their messages had been over the people's heads, they would have missed both heads and hearts.

Preaching Materials for the Prophets

"What shall I preach about?" is a question every preacher faces when he realizes that inevitably Sunday is coming. The prophets might have the answer. These men had sources from which they drew material in their sermon preparation, beyond the fact that they were what someone has called "God-intoxicated" men and men of incessant prayer.

Many prophets drew some of their sermon material from the revelation of God in nature. When men like Amos and Micah meditated deeply while in the solitude of God's wide open fields and under God's starry skies, the heavens declared the glory of God to them (Psalm 19:1). It produced preaching as rugged as the mountains, as broad as the horizon, as clear as sunshine.

Some prophets were brilliant students of the writings of Moses and the writing prophets of earlier centuries. Jeremiah and Ezekiel both came from priestly ancestors, and they grew up in homes where such writings were available. The influence of the older prophets on them is easily discernable in their recorded sermons. It is natural that such students should have preached on profound doctrines such as the majesty of God, the sinfulness of sin, repentance, the grace of God, salvation, love of God, and judgment. The so-called literary prophets—Isaiah, Jeremiah, Ezekiel, Hosea, Zechariah, and so forth—were the most influential men of their generations, and they have been profoundly influential in all the centuries since their times.

The writings of the prophets had a literary quality which indicated their thorough education. Some of them were gifted poets. Some were masters of the study of ethics. Most of them were familiar with history. Those who knew history knew how God had judged various nations and various people for various ways of life. Therefore, they could foresee and foretell the judgments of God which would come upon those who lived under similar conditions. Almost all of them were masters of theology, a subject which is called the "queen of the sciences."

Such prophets as Isaiah, Jeremiah, Amos, Micah, and Habakkuk were discerning students of international relations, current events, and national trends. Men like Ezekiel were students of people. "He sat where they sat," beside the river Chebar; that is, he saw life from their point of view and could understand their problems. From that viewpoint he could comfort, encourage, allay fear, counsel, and instruct. Since he understood them so well, he could preach to them intelligently, sympathetically, and helpfully.

Whatever else may be said about the prophets, they were not what someone has called "preacherettes preaching sermonettes to Christianettes." It is certain that they were never dull. No real prophet of God needs ever to get into a rut in his preaching, becoming as monotonous as a child playing on a piano with one finger. Sermons can come like telegrams, not like reading last week's newspaper. With all the vast material for preaching which may be found—in the Bible, in books, in nature, in current events, in the life problems of the people—preaching can be made dynamic, prophetic, if sufficient time and study and prayer are given to the preparation of sermons. The more exalted and demanding the task, the more exacting the preparation and delivery of sermons should be. "Quick-mix" sermons are neither very appetizing nor very nourishing to those who are hungry for spiritual food.

FOR BIBLE STUDY AND DISCUSSION

1. When can we have assurance that our message will not be in vain?
2. Mention some Scripture passages which may encourage a preacher in times of difficulty, opposition, or despair.
3. Discuss: "To preach prophetically necessitates that one live dangerously."
4. Do you feel that the growing complexity of the preacher's work is a wholesome trend? Give reasons for your answer. What suggestions can you give for solving this problem.
5. Discuss the prerequisites of a prophet—then and now.
6. Answer the question as completely as you can: "What shall I preach about?"

CHAPTER THREE

PREACHING DURING NATIONAL CRISES

> "Thus saith the Lord unto me; Go and stand in the gate of the children of the people, whereby the kings of Judah come in, and by the which they go out, and in all the gates of Jerusalem;
>
> "And say unto them, Hear ye the words of the Lord, ye kings of Judah, and all Judah, and all the inhabitants of Jerusalem."
>
> —Jeremiah 17:19-20

Under God, the prophets were the builders and saviors of their nation. Moses founded the theocracy. Samuel founded the monarchy. Ezekiel reorganized the nation out of the chaos of Babylonian captivity. A business man said to a preacher, "You preachers should stay out of the affairs of the state or nation. Politicians should run the government and preachers should attend to church affairs." The preacher replied, "Then we should tear out of the Bible most of the preaching of the Old Testament prophets."

A prophet of God should sit as it were on a lookout point and observe everything that degrades or destroys the moral and spiritual life of the people and the nation. If there is evil, he should become a troubler and disturber, as was Elijah (I Kings 18:17). Preachers who have prophetic judgment may take national crises as golden opportunities to preach social righteousness or social reform or heart-felt repentance or national humility before God.

Crises Inspire Prophetic Preaching

Much of the greatest preaching by the Old Testament prophets was inspired by some national or international crisis. The prophets analyzed causes of crises, predicted impending doom, and outlined the way of national wisdom. They preached authoritatively about the administrative policies of their governments whenever they involved moral integrity, social righteousness, legal justice, national security, or the personal influence of the rulers over the people. They were criticized as "political preachers," as was Amos (Amos 7:12-13), and were asked "to resign." But they preached on.

Old Testament history is full of illustrations of how God prepared and called brave men to prophesy for him in time of a national crisis. Moses set the example for all the prophets who came after him. He did not hesitate to strive with Pharaoh about granting freedom to the Israelites. Hosea said of him: "By a prophet the Lord brought Israel out of Egypt, and by a prophet was he preserved" (Hosea 12:13).

Samuel became the "strong man" of his nation during the crisis of the period of transition from the leadership of the judges to the rulership by the kings. He reorganized the nation, and he bound Israel to God through his prayers and his godly leadership. He lifted the standards of the people for peaceful living, for personal purity, and for sincerity of worship.

Elijah burst into the life of Israel like a sweeping tornado—bold, zealous, fiercely denunciatory of evil men and idolatrous practices. He was not timid about opposing King Ahab and Queen Jezebel concerning the introduction of idolatry into the land. He preserved the nation from Baalism and its fateful effects. Modern prophets can imitate him by striving to turn men from their shrine of worship at the national bank or the restaurant. Modern Jezebels need to be turned from worshipping at the dress shop or some place of worldly pleasure.

Amos was like an ancient edition of *U.S. News and World Report,* with the Spirit of God as the editor. He had been trained in the theological school of solitary communion with God while he tended flocks and gathered sycamore fruit (Amos 7:14). He became internationally minded through contacts with caravans of people who came from all over the known world to trade. He used a survey of the sins of other nations as a plan of approach, and then moved into denunciatory preaching about unholy conditions prevailing in Israel. It was not his type of prophetic preaching to say "peace, peace" when there was no peace. With rugged boldness Amos proclaimed to Israel the moral law of God upon which a nation must be built if it endures.

They are dark days always for any nation when there is no prophet in the land in the time of crisis. Every national ruler—be he king or prime minister or president—needs a prophet who can stand by him and advise with a "Thus saith the Lord." History has no more inspiring picture of a spiritually-minded preacher-statesman advising and encouraging a king in a national crisis than the story of how Isaiah was the stabilizing influence with Hezekiah when Jerusalem was being beseiged by the mighty army of Assyria (Isaiah 37).

Isaiah was fitted admirably to be an incisive thinker and interpreter of internal national affairs, to be the trusted adviser of kings. He took every opportunity to warn the king against putting any trust in Assyria, and to urge him not to have any confidence in Egypt. He bitterly denounced the folly of the king when he showed all his treasures and military might to the Babylonians (Isaiah 39). With daring faith Isaiah predicted a Messiah who would save the nation and who would set up an ideal social order (Isaiah 2, 7, 9, 11).

Jeremiah spent most of his prophetic ministry preaching about Judah's foreign policy toward nations such as Assyria, Egypt, and Babylon. He was called of God to the specific task of preaching on international affairs.

> "Behold, I have put my words in thy mouth. See, I have this day set thee over the nations and over the kingdoms, to root out, and to pull down, and to destroy, and to throw down, to build, and to plant."
>
> —Jeremiah 1:9-10

No braver prophet ever preached than did Jeremiah during the tragic decline and dissolution of his nation. For many years he preached on national affairs, fearlessly denounced the kings for their foolhardiness, and unceasingly urged the leaders to hear and heed the word of God. His mighty preaching fell on deaf ears, for the record does not tell that he ever won a single convert. At times he became woefully discouraged but he did not resign.

As crisis after crisis arose, prophet after prophet arose to preach the word of the Lord about them. Nahum vigorously denounced Nineveh. Zephaniah declared that his nation had come to a day of wrath, a day of distress and trouble, a day of danger that her high towers would be assaulted (Zephaniah 1:15-16). Ezekiel, Daniel, and Isaiah lived in the dark night of captivity, but they pointed to signs on the horizon which gave hope for the sunrise of national redemption. Their optimism which was born of faith is worthy of emulation.

The United States has faced continual crises during the past generation—three wars, a disastrous depression, the aggression of Communism, the repeal of the prohibition law with a subsequent flooding of the country with alcoholic beverage, racial disturbances, atomic dangers, a cold war, strained relations with national allies, frequent strikes, and many other problems. The prophets of the Old Testament times used such crises as golden opportunities to point people back to God and to interpret his holy will.

A Prophet's Purpose in Preaching during a National Crisis

True prophets have a profound conviction that God on his throne is sovereign, overruling the sinful follies of men and determining the destinies of nations (Psalm 2). They seek to discern and interpret the purposes of God in allowing these crises to come. They are world statesmen and believe that godly people should be world citizens.

The prophets were patriots, but they were not narrow nationalists. All of the prophets of Israel believed that their nation was elected of God to be the benefactor to other nations, the spiritual teacher, the harbinger of godliness and peace.

Is this not true of any nation which God allows to rise into world leadership? It does not take profound scholarship in history to see that such is true in the

United States of America. One can see the events of history throughout the Christian era pointing like the finger of God to America. The movement of Christianity westward from Jerusalem rather than eastward, the defeat of the Saracens at Tours in A.D. 722, which prevented Western Europe—and consequently America—from becoming Mohammedan in religion and culture, the victory in the Revolutionary War, and the preservation of the Union, all were crises in which God seemed to be working toward some noble purpose for this nation. Three destiny-determining events which transpired within less than a century seem to indicate what that purpose is. First, printing was discovered about A.D. 1450, and tradition says that the Bible was the first book to be printed; next, Columbus discovered the western world in 1492; then, the Protestant Reformation began to sweep Western Europe in 1517. It seems as clear as sunshine that God was preparing Western Europe and the United States to send missionaries into all the world with the open Bible and religious freedom.

> "Judge of the nations, spare us yet,
> Lest we forget—lest we forget!"
> —Rudyard Kipling

Prophetic preaching in Israel reached an exalted peak when the missionary message was proclaimed. Isaiah declared that peace would come under the righteous rule of the Messiah, when "the earth shall be full of the knowledge of the Lord, as the waters cover the sea" (Isaiah 11:9). He pictured a glorious social order and spiritual life which his people would enjoy and through which they would bless the Gentiles (Isaiah 11:1-10). This would be true because "out of Zion should go forth the law, and the word of the Lord from Jerusalem"

(Isaiah 2:3). Is not the God of the nations giving to the United States of America that same missionary opportunity and consequent blessings now?

Tides That Undermine Can Be Swept Back

Another purpose of prophetic preaching in a time of national crisis is to sweep back the tides of immorality which undermine the foundations of personal character and national security. Today's increasing crime rate, fearful rate of divorce, ravages of the liquor traffic, prevalence of juvenile delinquency, and the fearful growth of godless materialism all challenge God-called prophets to herald the truth of the righteousness of Almighty God. Following the world wars and other crises, this nation needs a prophet, or thousands of prophets, to lay firm foundations for a spiritual order of life, just as Ezekiel built for the Jews a new order of life after the old order was wrecked by the Babylonian invasion and seventy years of captivity.

FOR BIBLE STUDY AND DISCUSSION

1. Is the average college and seminary graduate likely to be so well trained that he can think clearly about national affairs? Can he preach on them with discernment, discretion, and helpfulness?
2. How can a preacher deal with a moral principle involved in some national crisis without "preaching politics"?
3. How can a preacher speak on a political or governmental crisis without violating the principle of separation of church and state?
4. Discuss what you consider the most dangerous trend in present-day national life, and suggest how prophets can help turn back the tide.
5. Discuss the saying of Jesus, "Render unto Caesar the things which are Caesar's; and unto God the things that are God's," in the light of the preaching by the prophets as discussed in this chapter.

CHAPTER FOUR

PROTESTING AGAINST SOCIAL UNRIGHTEOUSNESS

> "Let judgment [justice, ASV] run down as the waters, and righteousness as a mighty stream."
> —Amos 5:24

> "He hath shown thee, O man, what is good; and what doth the Lord require of thee, but to do justly, and to love mercy, and to walk humbly with thy God?"
> —Micah 6:8

It takes conviction, character, and courage to fulfill the duties of a true prophet. Prophets who follow in the train of Isaiah, Jeremiah, Amos, and Micah must have the unflinching courage which can be built only upon convictions as deep as one's soul. Such courage can be maintained only by a character which is built on faith in God. That type of courage is everlastingly essential when a preacher attacks social unrighteousness. The unrighteous people feel that they are being attacked personally, and they fight back. A social reformer must put on the whole armor of God, especially the girdle of truth, the breastplate of righteousness and the sword of the Spirit (Ephesians 6:14-17).

The Foundation of Social Righteousness Is Theological

Deep convictions against social unrighteousness are based on deep convictions about the righteousness of God. The burden of an enslaved nation came upon the heart of Moses in full force through the experience he had with God at the burning bush on Mt. Horeb (Exodus 3:1-10).

The mighty heart-power behind Isaiah's preaching against unrighteousness was his sense of the majesty and holiness of God. He saw the Lord in the temple, high and lifted up, with the seraphim singing "Holy, holy, holy, is the Lord of hosts: and the whole earth is full of his glory" (Isaiah 6:3). Thereafter, Jehovah was ever the "holy one of Israel" to him. After a vision like that, no preacher could ever be insensible to the woeful oppression of the poor by the greedy, or indifferent to the perverted justice in the courts of the land where verdicts were bought and sold, or without resentment against the haughty arrogance of the rich ladies as well as the men. The memory of that exalted vision was a constant reminder that God was righteous, and his character demanded righteousness in men.

Amos was one of the mightiest preachers of social righteousness of all times. He loosed blistering sermons like lightning flashes against covetousness, dishonesty, inhumanity toward the poor, perverted justice, and immorality. The people were either insensible to, or antagonistic toward, the Lord of Hosts. He cried out with all his soul for the people to prepare to meet God (Amos 4:12), to seek the Lord and live (Amos 5:6). It is no wonder. To him righteous Jehovah was universally sovereign; to him such a God demanded rightful dealings of men with men.

The dominant theme of his sermons, "Let justice roll down like the waters," is a superior text for prophetic preaching today.

It was Hosea's intense love for God which made him so fierce and intense in his denunciation of the sins which outraged the love of God, and which made him plead so tenderly for men to repent.

Ezekiel's pastoral ministry of encouragement and reproof and inspiration began with his vision of God, a vision of his purity, majesty, and glory (Ezekiel 1:28). Consequently he condemned the current sins of his people, such as promiscuity among the sexes, oppression of the poor, laxness of the law, all spawned by forgetfulness of God.

Possibly the social sins so prevalent in America today are due partially to the lack of deep, earnest, prophetic preaching on the holiness and righteousness of God. The nation needs more preachers like Amos, Hosea, Micah, and Isaiah. The country's newsstands are full of vulgar literature, its business is plagued with dishonesty, its schools are all too full of cheating, its homes are increasingly full of worldliness and drunkenness, its picture shows and television programs are laden with lewdness and crime, its family altars are decaying, and its pulpits are offering entirely too much apathetic and irrelevant preaching.

Social Sins Specifically Condemned by Name

All too many pulpit gestures are made by widespreading arms rather than by pointed fingers. The Old Testament prophets were not given to preaching vague generalities; they called sins by their names. They were not like hunters using shotguns which scatter the shot;

41

they used high-powered rifles. For instance, they made continual attacks on the two sins of sexual immorality and alcoholic drink, the sins which have been like twin cancers eating the hearts out of all the great civilizations which have collapsed. Hosea said, "Whoredom and wine and new wine take away the heart" (Hosea 4:11). He sobbed out the scathing indictment: "By swearing, and lying, and killing, and stealing, and committing adultery, they break out, and blood toucheth blood" (Hosea 4:2. See also 6:10, 7:4-5). Hosea gave the basic reason for all this iniquity: "For Israel has forgotten his Maker" (Hosea 8:14).

Early in his prophecy Isaiah began to denounce specific sins such as insincere worship, bribery, idolatry, unjust oppression, greed for land, and addiction to strong drink (Isaiah 1:11, 23; 2:8, 18; 3:14-15; 5:8, 11, 22). He denounced the drinking of alcohol, using almost nauseating language to picture the revolting spectacle of drunken priests and false prophets (Isaiah 28:7-8).

Listen to Habakkuk: "Woe unto him that giveth his neighbor drink, that putteth thy bottle to him, and makest him drunken also, that thou mayest look on their nakedness!" (Habakkuk 2:15). Did they have cocktail parties then?

It is a grave question whether or not the liquor consumption and sexual immorality in Jerusalem needed prophetic condemnation more than they do today in Washington, Chicago, New Orleans, San Francisco, and other places throughout the nation. In this day when sexual promiscuity and drunkenness have reached such a dreadful stage, a preacher cannot feel remotely that he is doing prophetic preaching unless he is crying out in no uncertain language against these horrible enemies of personal morality and national security. May God give America prophets who will dare to declare the physical death, sociological disaster, economic wreckage, moral and spiritual doom, which drunkenness and adultery inevitably will bring. May God save us from a "cocktail culture" in a society which must have an alcoholic drink to keep from being bored.

Demands for Social Righteousness

When Walter Rauschenbusch (d. 1918) began writing books about the social emphasis of the gospel of Jesus, there arose a division of thought about whether the gospel of Christ was a personal gospel or a social gospel. Those in both schools of thought have come to realize that there is only one gospel of Christ, with both personal and social applications. These two elements are like the two halves of an orange, each needed to make a perfect whole. Old Testament prophets preached both a right relation to God and a righteous relation with one's fellowmen. When a man's heart is regenerated by the Holy Spirit he has a new capacity and a new inner urge for righteous and peaceable relations with other people.

The prophets of Israel cried out for justice in the courts and fairness between people. They bemoaned the fact that verdicts in court trials were a marketable commodity that could be bought or sold by bribery. "Therefore the law is slacked, and judgment [justice] doth never go forth: for the wicked doth compass about the righteous; therefore wrong judgment proceedeth" (Habakkuk 1:4). When justice to all is not meted out impartially by the law of the land, it destroys one of the divinely built foundations of a righteous social order.

A social sin which was prevalent in Judah and Israel,

a sin which aroused the prophets to indignant denunciation, was that of accursed greed for land and money.
They were not inveighing against private ownership nor
were they advocating socialism. They preached against an
economic order which fostered mortgages and such heavy
taxation that poor people were reduced to practical slavery. The merchants had two standards of measurement, a
big measure to buy with and a small one to sell by. Worse
than that, they put the bad wheat on the bottom of the
bushel measure and the good on the top (Amos 8:5-6).

Isaiah was genuinely aroused. When greed of gain and
covetousness were sapping the moral strength of the people and the nation, he thundered:

> "Ye have eaten up the vineyard; the spoil of the poor is in
> your houses. What mean ye that ye beat my people to pieces,
> and grind the faces of the poor? saith the Lord God of Hosts."
> —Isaiah 3:14-15

> "Woe unto them that join house to house, that lay field to
> field, till there be no place."
> —Isaiah 5:8

Micah was equally as indignant:

> "They covet fields, and take them by violence; and houses,
> and take them away: so they oppress a man and his house, even
> a man and his heritage."
> —Micah 2:2

> ". . . who pluck off their skin from off them, and their flesh
> from off their bones; who also eat the flesh of my people, and
> flay their skin from off them; and they break their bones, and
> chop them in pieces, as for the pot, and as flesh within the
> caldron."
> —Micah 3:2-3

Is not materialism in the present world as vicious and
idolatrous as it was in the days of the prophets? Merchants

who put the rotten apples on the bottom of the basket and who fix their scales to make things heavier are not unheard of in most any town. Just how much is the desire for better business relations a dominant motive for affiliation with the church? Are not the deeds of greedy grafters and methods of dishonest profiteers today as worthy of pulpit denunciation as ever? An ungodly economic order, where the rich grow richer by excessively large profits and the poor grow poorer because of inadequate wages, is a challenge to a sympathetic prophet to preach the remedy by outlining the Scriptural principles of Christian stewardship.

In a capitalistic society a prophet who follows the pattern of preaching set by the Old Testament prophets must warn people against the idolatry of money-worship, against the deceitfulness of riches, against excessive love for the mammon of unrighteousness. Worship of money is a form of practical atheism. Neither the prophets nor Jesus taught that money itself was evil. They taught that the evil of it was the wrong desire for money, or the wrong method of acquiring money, or the wrong use of money. No man is better spiritually than his attitude toward money and material things which money can buy.

Social Sins Often Begin with Unrighteous Leadership

It may cost the life of a prophet if he attacks the sinful leadership of kings or priests or false prophets. The Old Testament prophets boldly and bravely did so, if they felt that the private life or public policies of a leader led others into unrighteousness.

When Ahab used his authority as king to have Naboth

stoned in order to get possession of his vineyard, Elijah's righteous indignation led him into a bitter denunciation of the iniquity of the king, and to prophesy Ahab's destruction (I Kings 21).

Isaiah placed the blame on the princes and elders when the poor were plundered, the innocent were declared guilty, and the guilty were allowed to go free. He excoriated the false prophets.

> "Therefore the Lord will cut off from Israel head and tail, branch and rush, in one day. The ancient and honorable, he is the head; and the prophet that teacheth lies, he is the tail. For the leaders of this people cause them to err; and they that are led of them are destroyed."
>
> —Isaiah 9:14-16

Priests and prophets who were getting drunk on alcoholic beverages were exposed without pity and condemned without reservation (Isaiah 28:7). Micah preached against the same evils which Isaiah deplored. He was unrestrained in condemnation of hypocritical priests and false prophets for their abuse of their offices, for their flattery of the rich, and for their time-serving cry of peace when there was no peace (Micah 3:5-7).

Malachi's quarrel with the priests was that they corrupted the worship of God by offering blemished sacrifices, which were an insult to deity (Malachi 1:8-14). He thought the Temple had better be closed than to dishonor God before all the people, as they were doing.

The condemnation of unworthy leaders by the Old Testament prophets is a delicate and dangerous standard to follow, but it involves a sacred duty. It may lead to a fate like that suffered by John the Baptist when he condemned Herod and Herodias for their horrible example of illicit marriage. However, it may merit the praise of the Saviour, such as he gave John after he had been beheaded.

Accent the Positive

One excellent way to protest against social sins is to preach and practice positive social righteousness. The Kingdom of God is a positive social concept; Christianity is positively social in its outreach; Christian churches have been the Good Samaritan to the world in many ways.

Christianity has been the fountain source of such healing streams as hospitals, orphanages, mental institutions, homes for the aged and for the incurables, care for unwed mothers, settlement houses in the slums for the underprivileged, charity to the poor, Christian schools and colleges, and the world-wide foreign missionary movement.

With prophetic zeal like the godly men of old, Christian leaders have fought, and must continue to fight, such social sins as slavery, dueling, liquor, narcotics, prostitution, adultery, child labor, pornographic literature, race prejudice, divorce, and war.

FOR BIBLE STUDY AND DISCUSSION

1. What two great Old Testament commandments did Jesus quote, revealing both the personal and social aspects of the gospel? What one word includes it all? (Matthew 22:35-40).
2. What are some of the great social contributions made to the world exclusively by Christianity?
3. How rich does a Christian have a moral right to become? What Bible principle is the antidote for materialism?
4. What are the ten greatest and most dangerous social sins which are generally prevalent in America? How can Christians combat them?

CHAPTER FIVE

PROPHESYING DOWNFALL BECAUSE OF SPIRITUAL DECAY

> "O Jerusalem, wash thine heart from wickedness, that thou mayest be saved."
>
> —Jeremiah 4:14

It is prophetic preaching when a man of God warns people that the wages of sin is death. The Old Testament prophets from time to time foretold some defeat or disaster which was inevitable unless the nation repented. No nation or civilization has even fallen when the people were trying to be right with God.

The prophets were exercising patriotism of the highest quality when they were warning people against some impending doom because of their ungodliness. Such was the case when Amos saw God measuring Israel with a plumbline, showing that the nation was like a leaning wall which would collapse in due time (Amos 7:7-9). He saw the nation to be like a basket of overripe fruit, ready to rot away (Amos 8:2). His plea of warning was, "Seek ye the Lord, and ye shall live" (Amos 5:6). God's laws are inexorable. Hosea expressed it when he said, "They have sown the wind, and they shall reap the whirlwind" (Hosea 8:7). God's law is that whatsoever a man soweth he shall reap in kind, and the fruitage of sin is death.

Forgetting Jehovah

The basic sin against which the ancient prophets cried with frenzied zeal was that of forgetting God. Jeremiah lamented: "Can a maid forget her ornaments, or a bride her attire? yet my people have forgotten me days without number" (Jeremiah 2:32). Such forgetfulness of God is an expression of practical atheism.

Forgetfulness of God expresses itself in many different ways. There are people whom society calls good people, who are good to their children, do not beat their wives, pay their debts, and stay out of jail, but who leave God completely out of their lives. They take no time to worship God at church, they have no money to give to God's kingdom causes, they take no interest in studying God's Word, and they make no efforts to lead others to Christ. They are not wicked but are just plain ungodly. Others who have worshipped God at one time grow so accustomed to his blessings that they forget to give thanks. Still others cannot resist the influence of the ungodly crowd, so they conform to the fashion of worldliness or wickedness rather than be different from other people. When the experience of forgetting God conceives, it gives birth to sin: and sin when it is fullgrown, bringeth forth death (cf. James 1:15). The prophets of God were able, like good physicians, to discern the cause of Israel's spiritual illnesses, able to foretell the results if they were not checked, and able to prescribe the remedy. They knew that both personal and national downfall eventually would come from the infectious germ of forgetting God.

One symptom of having forgotten God is idolatry. It stirred the souls of the prophets when the people of Israel followed the nations round them in worship of Baal. The destruction of Baalism became a life and death issue with Elijah when he challenged the priests of Baal to a contest on Mt. Carmel. Baal was thought to be the god of fertility, not a god of morality. Worship of Baal appealed to the desires for abundant crops and large families. When the God of righteousness was left out, these desires led to covetousness and adultery, and both sins were committed in the name of religion. Then, as always, men became like the god they worshipped. Baal was a god utterly without a moral standard. The theology of the people determined their morals; erroneous worship led to an erroneous walk.

With withering sarcasm Isaiah compared impotent idols with omnipotent Jehovah (Isaiah 46:1-8), and attributed Judah's captivity to idolatrous worship. Jeremiah likewise attacked idolatry with devastating bitterness (Jeremiah 10:1-11), while he exalted Jehovah. In speaking for God he said, "My people have committed two evils; they have forsaken me the fountain of living waters, and hewed them out cisterns, broken cisterns, that can hold no water" (Jeremiah 2:13). Jeremiah saw that idolatry not only violated the first of the Ten Commandments but also two other teachings of Moses in Deuteronomy: first, they should have only one altar for pure worship (in Jerusalem, Jeremiah thought), and the people of Israel should not mix with other nations who worshipped foreign deities.

Ezekiel spoke the word of God to the elders of Israel, telling about the fate of those who turned away from Jehovah to worship idols:

> "Repent, and turn yourselves from your idols; and turn away your faces from all your abominations. For every one of the house of Israel, or the stranger that sojourneth in Israel, which separateth himself from me, and setteth up his idols in his heart, . . . I will set my face against that man, and will make him a

sign and a proverb, and I will cut him off from the midst of
my people."

—Ezekiel 14:6-8

Habakkuk railed against the folly and disaster of idolatry
(Habakkuk 2:18-20). In Zephaniah's time there was worship of the sun and moon, incense was burned to Baal,
and priests of heathen gods were supported. The prophet
vigorously warned that the fierce anger of God would
sweep the nation away like the wind blows chaff (Zephaniah 2:1-3).

There are no new sins, and none has gone out of style.
Baal is not dead; he has just changed clothing. In modern times sin may have changed its form, but it has not
changed in spirit and essence. This is particularly true of
idolatry.

Baalism of today may be over-anxiousness about prosperity, worship of wealth, or greed for gold. Baal often
goes to church. The New Testament says covetousness is
idolatry. It is sure idolatry when men worship the almighty dollar. The shrine of the god of gold is at the
national bank. The shrine of the god of fashion is at the
department store. The shrines of the god of pleasure are
scattered throughout the land. It becomes a shrine for
idol worship when a man puts himself or anything else
on the most exalted throne of his desire or endeavor.
Modern idolatry should stir prophets of God to their
highest intensity of horror and noblest efforts of attack,
just as Baalism did in days long ago.

Men without God may hunger and thirst for him without knowing what they desire. Augustine was right when
he said, "Thou hast made us for thyself, and we find no
rest until we find our rest in thee." When the truth is
known, worldly people are often desperately thirsty in

their souls for God, for the living God (Psalm 42:2). Prophets like Amos know that nothing less than God can satisfy that spiritual thirst.

> "And they shall wander from sea to sea, and from the north even to the east, they shall run to and fro to seek the word of the Lord, and shall not find it. In that day shall the fair virgins and the young men faint for thirst."
>
> —Amos 8:12-13

A true prophet of God draws constantly from the deeps of God's truth in order to give people the water of life.

Insincere Worship of Jehovah

Another sign of spiritual decay is insincerity of worship. Some who go through the motions of worship are rank hypocrites, having the form of godliness but denying the power of it. Others think they are self-sufficient, without need of God. Isaiah said, "Woe unto them that are wise in their own eyes, and prudent in their own sight" (Isaiah 5:21). Some others are formalists, satisfied with rituals, ceremonies, and liturgies, without deep spiritual experiences with God or without sincere moral purpose in their lives. Amos cried out against this kind of insincerity:

> "Come to Bethel, and transgress; at Gilgal multiply transgression; and bring your sacrifices every morning, and your tithes *after three years* [ASV, "every three days"] and offer a sacrifice of thanksgiving with leaven, and proclaim and publish the free offerings: . . . I hate, I despise your feast days, and I will not smell in your solemn assemblies. Though ye offer me burnt offerings and your meat offerings, I will not accept them: neither will I regard the peace offerings of your fat beasts."
>
> —Amos 4:4-5; 5:21-22

The prophet's message in essence was to have God in the

heart, for immorality inevitably follows in the wake of insincere religious pretense.

During the reign of King Uzziah the prophet Isaiah
saw that national prosperity was causing a disastrous decline of sincere worship, even while there were lavish
and numerous sacrifices being offered in the Temple, and
multitudes of people going to a multiplicity of meetings.

> "Bring no more vain oblations; incense is an abomination
> to me; the new moons and sabbaths, the calling of assemblies,
> I cannot away with; it is iniquity, even the solemn meeting.
> Your new moons and your appointed feasts my soul hateth:
> they are a trouble unto me; I am weary to bear them."
>
> —Isaiah 1:13-14

One wonders what Isaiah would say about the multiplicity of church meetings in a highly organized church
of today, where church work often is mistaken for the
spiritual work of the church. The thing that matters is
what God sees in the hearts of those who go to so many
church meetings. Isaiah preached that unbelief was the
basis of their sham religion, and that lack of faith in God
was sure to bring doom upon them (Isaiah 7:8-9).

Jeremiah deplored a hollow worship in the Temple.
The sacrifices became occasions of feasting on good roast
beef instead of days of repentance and renewal of vows
to God.

> "Put your burnt offerings unto your sacrifices, and eat flesh.
> I spake not unto your fathers, nor commanded them in the day
> that I brought them out of the land of Egypt, concerning burnt
> offerings and sacrifices: but this I commanded them, saying,
> Obey my voice, and I will be your God, and ye shall be my
> people: and walk ye in all the ways that I have commanded you,
> that it may be well with you."
>
> —Jeremiah 7:21-23

As a result of the perversion of the sacrifices from acts of
faith to acts of feasting, he predicted that the ark of the

covenant would be carried away, the Temple would be destroyed, the entire sacrificial system would be abandoned, and even that Jerusalem would fall. In spite of the dire predictions, the prophet sobbed out the invitation of God to be saved: "Return ye backsliding children, and I will heal your backslidings" (Jeremiah 3:22).

During Hosea's time of prophecy there was plenty of sacrifice, but in reality they had forgotten God. Their daily lives showed it, for they were given to swearing, lying, killing, stealing, adultery, and drunkenness—the fruits of their inner life (Hosea 4:1-2). The sins of the people were like sword stabs into the prophet's heart. For people to be within their hearts so insincere toward God and in their daily lives so viciously licentious was to Hosea like a wife being untrue to her husband (Hosea 4:18; Chap. 3).

The classic pronouncement about sincere and insincere worship was made by Micah. He said the popular forms of sacrifices, ceremonies, and rituals in which his people were imitating other people were an abomination to God. He proclaimed one of the most exalted of the Old Testament interpretations of what God desires from men:

> "Wherewith shall I come before the Lord, and bow myself before the high God? shall I come before him with burnt offerings, with calves of a year old? Will the Lord be pleased with thousands of rams, or with ten thousands of rivers of oil? Shall I give my firstborn for my transgression, the fruit of my body for the sin of my soul?
> "He hath showed thee, O man, what is good; and what doth the Lord require of thee, but to do justly, and to love mercy, and to walk humbly with thy God?"
>
> —Micah 6:6-8

These old prophets got to the heart of the matter by requiring that worship come from the heart; the heart of

55

worship must be from the heart of the worshipper. Man can offer God nothing that will be acceptable to him unless it is given from a heart of genuine repentance, sincere love and worthy worship.

One of the heavy burdens on a modern prophet's heart is how to promote sincere and spiritual worship even by those who attend preaching services. When the piercing eye of God looks beyond other motives for church going, such as the influence of habit, the pleasure of social contacts, the loyalty to the pastor or class, or even motives which are more unworthy than these, just how much genuine sincerity of worship does he see in the hearts of the church-goers? It is a goal of a prophetic preacher to deliver a heart-warming message from God who is revealed in Christ, so that every worshipper will see God, will love God, and will go forth to serve God. Goldsmith expressed it beautifully:

> "Truth from his lips prevailed with double sway,
> And fools, who came to scoff, remained to pray."
> —The Deserted Village

Call for Repentance and Faith

A present-day preacher can never be more certain that he is walking in the path blazed by the prophets than when he is calling for sincere repentance of sin, for soul-gripping faith in God, and for humble worship before the throne of Deity. From the time of the dynamic and spirit-filled preaching of Joel during the eighth century before Christ until the tender tones of Christ were heard in Galilee, the prophets declared that God expects men to repent in their minds and hearts if they expect salvation. Joel said:

"Therefore also now, saith the Lord, turn ye even to me with all your heart, and with fasting, and with weeping, and with mourning: and rend your heart, and not your garments, and turn unto the Lord your God."

—Joel 2:12-13

The prophets knew that sin is a corrupting, killing foreign substance in the soul like a splinter in the hand. It brings festering, pain, and poison. The hurt cannot be healed until the cause of it is removed.

If a preacher wants to stir up his heart on Saturday night so he can preach prophetically on Sunday morning, let him walk up and down some hallway, reading aloud such passages on repentance as may be found in the fourth to sixth chapters of Amos, the fourteenth chapter of Hosea, the fourth and fifth chapters of Jeremiah, and the eighteenth chapter of Ezekiel. It will help any preacher to imbibe the spirit of John the Baptist who boldly exhorted people to bring forth fruits meet for repentance.

No preaching can have a piercing, prophetic quality which does not warn about the doom of forgetting God, which does not call for repentance for sin and faith in Christ to save.

FOR BIBLE STUDY AND DISCUSSION

1. Discuss which nations at one time during the Christian era have been most prominent in international affairs, but have fallen into mediocre power. In each case what sin has been most outstanding in causing the nation's downfall?
2. What is the most dangerous symptom that the people of America are forgetting God—worship of money? pleasure madness? drunkenness? home-breaking and divorce? crime? Sabbath-breaking? or what?
3. How can a pastor best promote humble, spiritual, sincere worship at the preaching service on Sunday morning?
4. Is either "quitting your meanness" or "doing better" identical

with repentance? Define and contrast reformation, remorse, penance, godly sorrow for sin, repentance.

5. How was genuine repentance brought about and how was it manifested in the following Bible characters—Job? David? Isaiah? Peter? Paul? Zacchaeus? The Philippian jailer?

CHAPTER SIX

PROCLAIMING THE LOVE OF GOD

> "For as the heaven is high above the earth, so great is his mercy toward them that fear him. As far as the east is from the west, so far hath he removed our transgressions from us. Like as a father pitieth his children, so the Lord pitieth them that fear him."
>
> —Psalm 103:11-13

Love is the greatest thing in the world, declared Henry Drummond in his delightful discussion of I Corinthians 13, Paul's matchless ode on love. Love also is the greatest thing in heaven, for God is love (I John 4:8). Love begins with God, and all true love is derived from him. No message which comes from God is complete without a winsome and persuasive presentation of some truth about the everlasting love of the Heavenly Father.

Jesus summed up in the one word love the teachings of Moses and the other prophets about the heaven-approved relations of men toward God and of men toward other men (Matthew 22:37-40; Deuteronomy 6:5; Leviticus 19:18, 34). Preaching the doctrine of the boundless and everlasting love of God the Father will be used of the Holy Spirit to bring men to repentance, to inspire faith, to encourage holiness, and to spread happiness in human hearts. What the Saviour preached in fullest perfection the prophets preached with growing perception and increasing power.

Preaching the Love of God

A preacher can herald a gospel of forgiveness and love, if he is living near to the heart of the God of love. That is why the preaching prophets of Old Testament times were so dynamic. It would be enlightening indeed to listen in on an old-fashioned testimony meeting where each prophet answered the question, "Why were you so concerned to lead people into intimate fellowship with God, and where did you get the content of your sermons which you preached with such authoritativeness?" One can imagine some of the answers.

While Moses was in Pharaoh's court, he saw the oppression of his people by a pagan nation of people who knew nothing about love. Their pagan religions only led them to become unspeakably cruel toward the enslaved Israelites. During forty years of intimate communion with God while he was in the wilderness, Moses felt with an ever-increasing conviction that God loved his people (Exodus 3:7-9). He felt that God had the jealousy of true love, and his beloved should return his love with heart, soul and might (Deuteronomy 6:5, 15). It soon dawned upon him that if God loved his people so, it obligated them to love their fellowmen—even to love strangers—as they loved themselves. So Moses returned to Egypt with a heavenly fire in his heart and a heavenly message on his tongue. Until his dying day he preached, "The eternal God is thy refuge, and underneath are the everlasting arms" (Deuteronomy 33:27).

Where did Hosea get materials for his sermons? The fountain source of his preaching was the love of God.

Out of a tragic experience with the frailty of human love he found that only in God does one find a love from which nothing can separate us (Romans 8:38-39). He married Gomer, the sweetheart of his youth, and was a devoted husband to her. But alas, to his soul-crushing sorrow, she was unfaithful to him. Although she went to the depths of infidelity and depravity, Hosea could not shake off his undying love for her. He forgave her. He took her out of her debauchery; he took her back to his heart and home. When life around him was darker than midnight, he looked toward heaven and saw a light. It was the face of God, bright with forgiving grace and radiant with yearning love. He could never forget that look.

Hosea knew that the people of his nation were as unfaithful to his loving God as his adulterous wife had been to him (Hosea 4:12-13; 7:3-8). Yet, God taught him that if he could love and forgive Gomer, surely Jehovah could love an unfaithful people and forgive those who repent. The compassionate prophet cried out persuasively that God is love, that God would forgive their gross unfaithfulness, if they would return unto the Lord (Hosea 6:1). He tried to touch their hearts by reminding them how God loved them when Israel was a young nation. God so graciously led Israel out of Egypt, taught them like teaching a baby to walk, healed them of their diseases, drew them with the cords of love (Hosea 11:4). Hosea preached to them about the gracious Jehovah whose heart was breaking for them, who was saying, "How shall I give thee up, Ephraim? . . . I will not execute the fierceness of mine anger, I will not return to destroy Ephraim: for I am God, and not man" (Hosea 11:8, 9).

Amid the gloom that fell when King Uzziah died,

Isaiah went into the sanctuary to seek the light (Isaiah 6:1-8). Behold, he saw the Lord of hosts, the King of kings. Isaiah was never the same after that experience. When he saw God's glory, he confessed his sins. In infinite grace God forgave the prophet's sin and cleansed him from his iniquity. Thereafter, Isaiah preached that Jehovah was a God of grace and love, giving strength to the needy, refuge from the storms, shade in which to hide from burning suns, feasts for the famished. He promised that God would wipe away the tears from the eyes of those who sorrow and would swallow up death in victory (Isaiah 25).

Jeremiah had no miraculous vision of God and his seraphim, such as Isaiah experienced. While he was in his priestly father's house at Anathoth, near Jerusalem, he read the soul-stirring messages of Hosea declaring in soft and appealing words that God hates sin violently but that he loves sinners tenderly. The tender-hearted Jeremiah became conscious of the Divine Presence speaking to him like one friend to another. God was calling him to prophesy to the nations (Jeremiah 1:5-10). His shrinking soul trembled when God commissioned him to attack the citadels of sin, to root up the seed of iniquity, to tear down the temples of idolatry, and to prophesy the doom of his beloved nation. That would have been intolerable to him but for the fact that God also commissioned him to build and to plant. He joyously announced to Judah that God said of her people, "Yea, I have loved thee with an everlasting love: therefore with lovingkindness have I drawn thee. . . . Is Ephraim my dear son? is he a pleasant child? . . . I will surely have mercy on him" (Jeremiah 31:3, 20).

When Isaiah was prophesying, the people of Judah

were dejected and despairing, enduring exile from their beloved Jerusalem and bondage to the Babylonians. They were bowed down in discouragement, sitting down and weeping beside the rivers and canals of that country (Psalm 137). The prophet's heart was almost breaking in sympathy. In seeking a way of comfort and salvation for them, Isaiah turned to God. In the night he, through faith, saw a light. Through divine revelation he saw salvation both for the nation and for individuals, a salvation made possible through the Suffering Servant of Jehovah. Through the telescope of faith he saw the Suffering Servant wounded for men's transgressions; he saw that by his stripes men could be healed (Isaiah 49-53).

The Spirit of God commissioned Isaiah to preach the good news of the Suffering Servant's love. He preached the gospel of salvation for the poor. He proclaimed deliverance to those in spiritual bondage as well as to those in physical slavery. He joyously promised power to open the eyes which are blind to heavenly truth. He announced to the people that the day of salvation was already there (Isaiah 61:1-2; 62:11).

The prophets one and all were preachers of theology, the theology of a God of love and forgiveness. Moses preached this gospel, Micah heralded it forcefully, Isaiah proclaimed it eloquently, Jeremiah sobbed it at one breath and shouted it at the next, Hosea sweetened it, and Isaiah sang it in poetic beauty. Who follows in their train?

Preaching Christ, God's Gift of Love

God so loved that he gave. By peering into the future by faith in the God with whom they had daily fellowship, the prophets preached Christ Jesus as savior, the unspeakable gift of God's love. What else could be the central theme of preaching today, if it is to be prophetic preaching? The coming Messiah was to the gospel of the prophets like the central nerve that runs through the spinal column, like the melody of a song which may be played with a multiplicity of variations, like the light of the sun of which all other lights are but reflections. "And beginning at Moses and all the prophets, he expounded unto them in all the scriptures the things concerning himself" (Luke 24:27).

The prophets promised in their sermons that the Messiah would come. Moses said, "The Lord thy God will raise up unto thee a Prophet from the midst of thee, of thy brethren, like unto me; unto him ye shall hearken" (Deuteronomy 18:15). Samuel (II Samuel 7:12) and Isaiah (11:1) and Jeremiah (Jeremiah 23:5) each predicted that the Messiah would be born of the line of David. Micah announced that the Saviour would be born in Bethlehem (Micah 5:2). Isaiah declared that it was the purpose of God to establish a kingdom of righteousness which would be ruled by the Prince of Peace (Isaiah 2:2-5). He would be born of a virgin, and his name would be Immanuel (Isaiah 7:14), Wonderful Counsellor, Mighty God, Everlasting Father, Prince of Peace (Isaiah 9:16). He would usher in a social order of righteousness and peace (Isaiah 11:1-9).

Jeremiah preached in great spiritual power about salvation through the coming Messiah. He was quite specific in foretelling many details about Jesus. He saw that the love of God was to be expressed through the righteous branch which God would raise up from the family tree of David (Jeremiah 23:5), and through a new covenant or contract about salvation which God would make (Jeremiah 31:31-32). Jesus explained this when he said at the institution of the Lord's Supper, "This cup is the new covenant in my blood" (I Corinthians 11:25 ASV).

Zechariah held aloft the torch of hope, and it burned with a new brightness. He affirmed that the Messiah would have priestly powers, making atonement for sins (Zechariah 6:12-13). He foretold that the Messiah would come victoriously but humbly, not riding a war horse like a military victor but riding the colt of an ass like an ambassador of peace (Zechariah 9:9).

Malachi foretold that the Messiah would have a forerunner (whom Jesus identified as John the Baptist), and that the Sun of righteousness would rise with healing in his wings (Malachi 3:1; 4:2).

It was Isaiah who rose to the loftiest heights of spiritual perception about the coming Messiah, who heralded his coming with the noblest eloquence and most heart-melting exhortation. He pictured in poetic but poignant language the Messiah's vicarious suffering for the iniquities and transgressions of sinful men.

If Christ is taken out of preaching, it deteriorates into mere social and ethical moralizations, at best. It loses the authority of the prophet's "Thus saith the Lord." Take Christ out of a prophet's sermons and they will lose the power of the Holy Spirit (John 16:14), they will lose their dynamic appeal (John 12:22), and they will fade like a feeble cry in the wind.

Preaching the Doctrines of Grace

Great preaching is not possible unless it proclaims great doctrines that grow out of the truth about a God of righteousness and love. Super-sensationalism or hyperemotionalism in preaching always fails to meet the needs of the human heart. A sin-burdened heart yearns for grace. The doctrine of the love of God is the root from which the flowers of all the doctrines of grace come. The theological doctrines about salvation—the doctrines of grace—were the steel framework on which the sermons of the prophets were built. Doctrinal truth about God's grace is the spinal column of prophetic preaching; moral and social righteousness is the flesh and blood of it; Christ is the heartbeat of it. A healthy body requires all three.

Out of the doctrine of the love of God flows the doctrines of conviction for sin, forgiveness conditioned on repentance, justification through faith, regeneration, sanctification, glorification, and other doctrines about the work of God in the human heart.

Conviction for sin was preached by all the prophets from Amos to Zechariah, that is, "from A to Z." Repentance was demanded by all from Moses to Malachi, from Jeremiah to John the Baptist. Regeneration, according to a new covenant of grace which was to be written in the hearts of individual men, was preached and promised by Jeremiah (Jeremiah 31:31-34). Ezekiel promised a new heart and a new spirit, as he pathetically implored the people to cast off their sins and not to die in them (Ezekiel 18:31-32). Sanctification was constantly the preaching theme of those men who yearned to see their beloved people adhere to the God of their fathers. Daniel sought to turn the eyes of the people heavenward for glorification:

> "And many of them that sleep in the dust of the earth shall awake, some to everlasting life, and some to shame and everlasting contempt. And they that be wise shall shine as the brightness of the firmament; and they that turn many to righteousness as the stars for ever and ever."
>
> —Daniel 12:2-3

The world does not hear enough of that kind of preaching, and it sorely needs it. Sinful men cannot pass from death unto life without repentance for sin, the forgiveness of God, and being transformed into His likeness by regeneration through the Holy Spirit.

FOR BIBLE STUDY AND DISCUSSION

1. Where did the various prophets first learn about God being a God of love? Moses? Hosea? Isaiah? Jeremiah?
2. Where else besides in the writing prophets do the Old Testament Scriptures teach about the Messiah?
3. At what times in Jewish history was the Messianic hope inflamed to the highest?
4. What mistaken ideas about the Messiah's coming and about his rule did Jesus have to overcome?
5. What was the all-inclusive concept and contribution to the world that Jesus came to give to men, which was the theme of his preaching from first to last?

CHAPTER SEVEN

PROMISING A GLORIOUS FUTURE

> "But unto you that fear my name shall the Sun of righteousness arise with healing in his wings."
>
> —Malachi 4:2

If one desires to preach like the prophets, he must be an optimist as well as a realist. Isaiah and Ezekiel and other giant-like preachers of the Old Testament voiced abounding optimism about a glorious future under the righteous rule of Jehovah. This was prophesied to come when the people turned from their unrighteousness and ungodliness to obey Jehovah of Hosts. Unless these prophets had preached this glorious hope for the future, they could not have exerted such profound influences upon their own and succeeding generations.

If preaching is to influence people to worship a God of holiness, to obey a God of righteousness and to love a God of grace, its message must reveal the spiritual results of such obedience and love. Preaching should do more than denounce the sinfulness of sin; it must also declare the eternal hope which is promised through Christ. Influential preachers combine inspiration with condemnation, combine acceptance of salvation with forsaking of sin, combine allurement to heaven with warning about hell, combine grace and mercy with retribution and judgment. Billy Sunday is quoted as having said about preaching: "Always leave some cookies on the bottom shelf."

Restoration of Nation Prophesied

The promise to the Jews that they would be returned from exile and restored to a happy life in their homeland was to them almost like the promise of heaven is to people today. Isaiah went quite beyond mere promise of restoration from captivity. He soared to the heights of abounding enthusiasm about the coming of an eternal ruler whose name should be Wonderful Counsellor, Mighty God, Everlasting Father, who would sit in majestic glory forever on the throne of David, and rule in righteousness as the Prince of Peace (Isaiah 9:1-7).

Even Jeremiah, who saw the darkest clouds on the horizon of the future, saw also the gray streaks of the light of a coming dawn piercing the darkness. With keen perception he saw that the captivity of Judah would last precisely seventy years (Jeremiah 29:10). Just as soon as he had predicted the seventy years of captivity, he promised liberation. The words of Jeremiah in Chapters 30-33 almost sound like the joyous and encouraging words of Isaiah (Isaiah 40-66), as they glow radiantly with hope and promise for the future. In Jeremiah's words concerning the future may be found the seed of the doctrines of the love of God the Father, the redemption made possible through the new covenant of grace which was to be sealed by the blood of God the Son, and the overflowing joys of the communion of God the Holy Spirit.

Hosea wept as he condemned the sins of the people of Judah, but he promised healing of their wounds if they of Zion would repent (Hosea 5:13; 6:1). He had a vision of a bright future. He held out a hope for the nation to blossom like a lily eventually, to become as beautiful as an olive tree, to be as verdant as growing grain (Hosea 14:4-7).

Amos thundered denunciation upon those who were guilty of social sins, but he was quick to declare that Jehovah was a forgiving God who would restore Israel. There would be flourishing cities, fruited fields, happy abundance (Amos 9:11-15).

A glorious Jerusalem was envisioned by Zechariah when he lifted up his eyes (Chapter 2). A young man with a measuring rod was told that the new Jerusalem was so large it could not be measured. It would not need a city wall for protection; God would be like a wall of fire about it and would be the glory in the midst of it (Zechariah 2:5). Jerusalem would be populated with contented old people living in peace (Zechariah 8:4), with happy children playing in the streets in safety (Zechariah 8:5), with prosperous people living in plenty (Zechariah 8:12). Even the bells on the harness of the horses and the rattling of kitchen utensils would sound forth the message of the holiness of the Lord (Zechariah 14:20-21). Jerusalem was the apple of God's eye (Zechariah 2:8).

Like the nostalgic exiles who sat down by the rivers in Babylon and wept for their beloved Jerusalem (Psalm 137), the hearts of modern men can find no assurance of salvation, no satisfying joy, no peace or hope, until they find them in God through Jesus Christ the Saviour. If a preacher follows the example of the prophets, he will herald in glowing terms the golden promises of the gospel of Christ. The ever-brightening hope which the Old Testament prophets preached was but the foregleam of the sunrise of the blessed hope which was revealed from God through Christ. The gospel of Christ offers such heavenly gifts as forgiveness of sin, cleansing of the conscience, power over temptation, joy in service, happiness in Christian fellowship, growth in Christlikeness, a triumphant victory over death, and eternal blessedness in heaven.

Hope Held Out to Remnant

It was to a remnant only that the prophets promised a glorious future, not to all of the people of Israel. The prophets were not "universalists"; they preached that only those who repented and put faith in God would be saved. They saw that it was a narrow way leading to salvation and comparatively few would find it.

The prophet Joel, early in the nation's history, spoke of a remnant that would be delivered, a remnant made up of those who would call upon the name of the Lord (Joel 2:32). Likewise, Amos declared that the Lord God of Hosts would bestow grace upon a remnant on condition that they would hate evil, love goodness, and see that justice to the people was meted out in their courts (Amos 5:15). Micah, a contemporary of Amos, not only foretold the restoration of the remnant but foresaw the remnant under God becoming a mighty missionary agency among the Gentiles (Micah 2:12; 4:7; 5:7-8). God's mightiest works often are done through God-called and consecrated minorities.

Comfort and Salvation Offered to People

Isaiah had a way of holding out the brightest hope during the darkest part of the night (Isaiah 10:17-22). When the future of the Jewish people seemed most barren, he predicted Israel's survival and salvation. He exalted a glorious Saviour. He predicted the Saviour's virgin birth and his meaningful name, Immanuel (Isaiah 7:14). He envisioned the salvation by this Saviour as being like people who are lost in darkness but see a great light. "The people that walked in darkness have seen a great light: they that dwell in the land of the shadow of death, upon them hath the light shined" (Isaiah 9:2).

Isaiah saw a perfect social order under the righteous rule of the Saviour, a Branch out of the rod of Jesse (Isaiah 11:1-9). He used ornate and vivid metaphors in describing the social order that would prevail under the Prince of Peace. He foresaw a warless world with men converting their instruments of war into implements of peaceful agriculture (Isaiah 2:5). In striking language he described this social order as a time when wolves and lambs would dwell together in peaceful accord, when cows and bears would eat peacefully together, when children would not be hurt while playing on a serpent's den, when the knowledge of the Lord would cover the earth like waters cover the depths of the sea (Isaiah 11:1-9). It was an alluring way to describe a heavenly ideal which is attainable under the glorious Saviour's righteous rule.

Isaiah was a prophet of salvation and comfort (Isaiah 40-66). It is said that for every person in a church pew today who needs correction and denunciation, there are ten persons who need comfort and love. In Chapters forty to sixty-six of Isaiah there are words of exquisite charm and infinite comfort. "Comfort ye, comfort ye my people, saith your God" (Isaiah 40:1) is as painfully appropriate and as dreadfully needed in pulpits today as ever in the history of God's dealings with men.

No passage in the Old Testament inspires a God-called preacher to herald the gospel more than these latter chapters in Isaiah. These words have in them a literary beauty like the beauty of the rainbow, majestic thought like the majesty of the mountains, a wideness of vision like the wideness of the sea, a flowing oratory like the rushing of Niagara, an awe-inspiring power like the flash of lightning across a storm-swept sky, a fragrant restfulness like a rose garden in full bloom, the spirit of worshipfulness like soft organ music in a dedicated sanctuary. The strength, power, and appeal of it all is the message of God's tender mercy, forgiving grace, and abundant salvation.

What an ideal for preaching!

Hope for Heaven Preached

Within every heart there is an unquenchable thirst for assurance of a better life to come. The human heart is weary of spiritual wanderings and it wants an eternal home. It despairs under continual disappointments. It is restive under the frailties of the flesh and with the illnesses that plague ·the body. There is an irrepressible faith that springs up continuously in the human heart, believing that there awaits a heaven where no sin abounds and no sorrow comes, a heaven of bliss in the presence of Deity and all his redeemed. Tennyson expressed it:

> "Thou wilt not leave us in the dust:
>   Thou madest man, he knows not why,
> He thinks he was not made to die;
>   And thou hast made him: thou art just."
>   —*In Memoriam*

The prophets believed in immortality with a growing perception and conviction about it. They had the Scripture about Enoch whom God took (Genesis 5:24). They treasured the last recorded words of Moses: "The eternal God is thy refuge, and underneath are the everlasting arms" (Deuteronomy 33:27). They knew how Elijah had been caught up in a chariot of fire and taken into heaven by a whirlwind (II Kings 2:11).

Among the earlier preaching prophets the idea of the future life was somewhat obscure and was mentioned only occasionally. The glory which they foresaw was principally the glory that would come to the nation Israel. Later, when Judah was in exile in Babylon the nation ceased to exist, and their hopes for the future became personal. In their thinking they made tremendous advances toward the New Testament conception of heaven, a heaven not on earth but in a transcendental sphere of bliss beyond death. The vision of heaven grew brighter.

Job believed in the affirmative when he asked his question, "If a man die, shall he live again?" (Job 14:14). He could boldly exclaim by faith, "I know that my redeemer liveth . . . in my flesh shall I see God" (Job 19:25-26). The Psalmist was assured of life in glory after death, when he said, "Thou shalt guide me with thy counsel, and afterward receive me in glory" (Psalm 73:24). Ezekiel's vision of the valley of dry bones dramatically revealed his belief in the resurrection (Ezekiel 37). Daniel saw beyond the resurrection an everlasting life where soul-winners would shine as stars for ever and ever (Daniel 12:2-3).

Jesus and the Apostles were inspired greatly by the teachings of the prophets about the resurrection and heaven. Jesus continually prophesied both. On the day of Pentecost Simon Peter quoted Psalm 16:10 to show that Christ rose from the dead according to prophecy (Acts 2:31). The Apostle Paul, in his incomparable discussion in I Corinthians 15 about the resurrection, was inspired to quote Isaiah 25:8 and Hosea 13:14 in his exultant outburst about the victory over death and the grave.

The author of Revelation was saturated in mind and heart with the teachings of the prophets about the ineffable joys of the future life in heaven. Much of the imagery of heaven as described in Revelation was taken directly from the Old Testament prophets. For example, the song "Holy, holy, holy" which was sung by the four-winged beasts that John saw before the throne (Revelation 4:8) was sung by the seraphim which Isaiah heard during his vision (Isaiah 6:1-8). An extended list of such references can be made.

Revelation 21:1, "A new heaven and a new earth," is taken from Isaiah 65:17 and 66:22.

Revelation 21:3, "The tabernacle of God is with men," is taken from Ezekiel 37:27.

Revelation 21:4, "God shall wipe away all tears from their eyes; and there shall be no more death, neither sorrow, nor crying, neither shall there be any more pain," is taken from Isaiah 25:8 and 35:10.

Revelation 21:23, "The city hath no need of the sun," is taken from Isaiah 60:19-20.

Revelation 21:24, "The nations of them which are saved shall walk in the light of it: and the kings of the earth do bring their glory and honor into it," is taken from Isaiah 60:3 and 49:23.

Revelation 21:25, "The gates of it shall not be shut at all by day: for there shall be no night there," is taken from Isaiah 60:11 and Zechariah 14:7.

Revelation 21:27, "And there shall in no wise enter into it anything that defileth," is taken from Ezekiel 44:9.

Revelation 22:1, "A pure river of water of life," is taken from Ezekiel 47:1, and Revelation 22:2, "The tree of life," is taken from Ezekiel 47:12.

Revelation 22:5, "And they shall reign for ever and ever," is taken from Daniel 7:18.

The only perfect criterion for preaching on heaven is found in him who said, "In my Father's house are many mansions. . . . I go to prepare a place for you. . . . that where I am, there ye may be also" (John 14:2-3). This discourse on heaven by him who came from heaven is doubtless the most beloved passage in all the New Testament. It is true because every heart in any congregation anywhere is hungry for assurance of heaven hereafter.

FOR BIBLE STUDY AND DISCUSSION

1. What Scriptures besides the prophetic writings made Israel expect a future King like David? Who announced to Mary that this was being fulfilled?
2. Has Zechariah's prophecy about a glorious Jerusalem ever been realized? Can his prophecy be used in present-day preaching?
3. What safe rule can be used in applying the prophecies of a restored Jerusalem to thinking and preaching about heaven?
4. What contribution did the Apostle Paul make to the hope for immortality, the second coming of Christ, and heaven?

CHAPTER EIGHT

PLEADING WITH MEN TO ACCEPT SALVATION

> "How beautiful upon the mountains are the feet of him that bringeth good tidings . . . that publisheth salvation."
>
> —Isaiah 52:7
>
> "Ho, every one that thirsteth, come ye to the waters, and he that hath no money; come ye, buy, and eat."
>
> —Isaiah 55:1

If the Old Testament prophets were preaching in churches today, what would they say? Doubtless they would be preaching on the same subjects identically that they were proclaiming six to eight centuries before Christ. They would be evangelists, preaching repentance and faith as the way of salvation, for they had a passion for souls. They would be evangelists with beautiful feet (Isaiah 52:7).

The hope of salvation through the coming Messiah was held up by the prophets like a torch through many, many years of midnight darkness. Prophets of today can make and should make the pathway to salvation clear to people in darkness, and as alluring as a flowery path in the springtime. A group of theological students vividly remember how George W. Truett stood in chapel and exhorted them in earnest and plaintive tones: "O young preachers, make it clear to people how to be saved; make it very clear how to be saved!" The evangelistic call telling men how to be saved through Christ is the heart-beat of prophetic preaching. "The testimony of Jesus is the spirit of prophecy" (Revelation 19:10). The rebukes voiced by the prophets, the warnings, the tears, the appeals, all revolved around the desire of God for people to be saved. To tell of God's love for lost souls is the supreme purpose of God for calling men into a prophetic ministry.

God Longing for Men to Be Saved

In the days of the Old Testament prophets, as well as now, there were people so foolish as to say, "God is too good to send anyone to hell." The prophet Ezekiel was quick to emphasize that God had no pleasure in the death of the wicked (Ezekiel 33:11). God longs for men to turn from their evil ways and to live. A discerning prophet of a loving God never gives people the impression that God hates sinners. God loves sinners with an undying love; it is death-dealing sin which God hates with a fierceness born of his righteous love. When a man himself chooses to reject God and thereby is lost, it should never be blamed on God. If he is separated from God by his own choice and dies, he is responsible, not God. After death men must live with their own choices (Revelation 22:11). Hosea implored: "O Israel, return unto the Lord thy God; for thou hast fallen by *thine* iniquity" (Hosea 14:1).

Prophets Praying for Sinners

A prayerless prophet is a powerless prophet. Although intercessory prayer is chiefly a priestly function, any prophet who loves people will implore God in agonizing prayer for lost people. Moses uttered a prayer for Israel which was selfless and passionate, wrung from a devout soul:

> "Moses returned unto the Lord and said, Oh, this people have sinned a great sin, and have made them gods of gold. Yet now, if thou wilt forgive their sin—; and if not, blot me, I pray thee, out of thy book which thou hast written."
>
> —Exodus 32:31-32

There are many other instances of Moses praying intercessory prayers (Exodus 34:9; Numbers 11:2, 14:19-20; Deuteronomy 9:18-26).

The prophet Samuel at Mizpah prayed for Israel until they confessed their sins to God (I Samuel 7:5-6). Jeremiah ranked Samuel next to Moses as an intercessor (Jeremiah 15:1).

Amid the imprecations and prophecies of doom made by Jeremiah he prayed that his eyes might be a fountain of tears. He wept day and night as he confessed his own sins as well as the sins of his people (Jeremiah 9:1; 14:7, 17-21).

After Habakkuk had surveyed the tragic conditions of morality and spirituality in his nation and the nations round about him, he flung himself at the feet of the Almighty in prayer for a revival of God's work in the midst of the years (Habakkuk 3:2).

Prophets Urging Men to Repent

The faithful prophets, almost without an exception, denounced sin and pleaded for repentance. A would-be prophet is strikingly unlike the mighty Prophet of Galilee if sin does not hurt him to the depths of his heart. The prophets of old usually had fire in their hearts but tears in their eyes when they denounced sin. They knew that unless a man was convicted of sin he would not implore

God for forgiveness. A prophet will put people to sleep while preaching about God's forgiveness unless first they are made conscious that they are in dreadful need of forgiveness.

Isaiah called sins by their well-known names; he charged people openly and fearlessly with corrupt business deals, harlotry, murder, alcoholic drinking, greed for land, thievery, bribery, injustice in the courts and other such sins. Likewise Jeremiah in his great Temple sermon (Jeremiah 7) denounced oppression of the poor, lack of justice in the courts, greedy violence, heathen worship, stealing, lying, murder, adultery, slander, and perjury. He predicted punishment for their sins, and asked, "What else can God do?" (Jeremiah 9:1-7). The same sort of specific name-calling of sins was true of Amos (Amos 4:1-5), Hosea (Hosea 4:11-19; 7:1-4), Micah (Micah 7:1-5), and many others.

Sinners need to be told by prophets about their sins and their need for forgiveness. There are personal sins and social sins, sins of omission and of commission, sins of profanity and of Sabbath breaking, sins of adultery and of drunkenness, sins of hating and of coveting, sins of sensuality and of gluttony, sins of lying and of swearing, sins of cheating in school and of cheating on income tax reports, sins of worshipping money and of forgetting God. Sin! sin! sin! Prophets of the most High God, with thunder in their voices like Amos but with tears in their eyes like Hosea and pain in their hearts like Jeremiah, tell people about the sinfulness of their sins and the destruction that comes therefrom, unless they repent.

Repentance is the most reasonable thing that God could require of one who sins. It was preached by the prophets much more frequently, it seems, than it is today.

Various prophets gave various reasons why men should repent. Amos called for repentance, demanding a "returning unto the Lord" (Amos 4:6, 8-11), or else they would come to judgment and destruction. Hosea extolled the love of God who would forgive sinners, even if their sins were as heinous as the sins of Gomer, his wife. He promised that if they repented God would heal their backsliding, would love them freely, would be to them like the fresh dew of the morning, would make them grow as a lily, would make them as beautiful as the olive trees, would cause them to grow as the corn or the vine (Hosea 14:4-7).

The doctrine of repentance, preached so lovingly and so eloquently by Hosea, was voiced persuasively by Isaiah and afterwards by Jeremiah. Isaiah pleaded, "Let the wicked forsake his way, and the unrighteous man his thoughts: and let him return unto the Lord" (Isaiah 55:6). Jeremiah reasoned practically, "Only acknowledge thine iniquity, that thou hast transgressed against the Lord thy God. . . . Turn, O backsliding children, saith the Lord; for I am married unto you" (Jeremiah 3:13-14).

This doctrine, preached so fervently and so insistently by the prophets, was repeated and reiterated by John the Baptist and Jesus. Surely a modern prophet can ill afford to relegate the doctrine to a minor place in his preaching.

Prophets Promising a New Heart

Early Old Testament prophets thought of Jehovah as belonging to the Hebrew nation exclusively, and preached national repentance. Since repentance must be experienced individually and with heartfelt sincerity, the prophets probed deeper and deeper into the individual soul-life. They preached less and less to men in general, more and more to a man in particular. They preached more and more frequently about personal repentance and faith and obedience, promising that the Lord would give them a new heart (Jeremiah 17:5-10). They got to the heart of the matter by seeking to persuade men to get right toward God in their hearts. After David was rebuked by the prophet Nathan, he cried, "Create in me a clean heart, O God" (Psalm 51:10).

With Jeremiah, a man's relation to God was determined by his spiritual attitudes, by repentance, faith, emotions, will, love. A man must bear the responsibility of his choices and sins. He could not put the blame on others or upon society; he could not say "the fathers have eaten sour grapes, and the children's teeth are set on edge" (Jeremiah 31:29). He preached that the law of God must be written on an individual's heart (Jeremiah 31:33). Jeremiah tersely avowed that it was no more possible for an individual to cleanse his heart from iniquity without the help of God than it was for an Ethiopian to change his color or a leopard to change his spots (Jeremiah 13:23). He declared that the Lord would give them a heart to know him, when they would return to him with their whole hearts (Jeremiah 24:7). God would put the law in their inward parts, and write it in their hearts (Jeremiah 31:33). Jehovah would give them one heart so that they would fear him forever and that they would not depart from him (Jeremiah 32:39-40).

Ezekiel took up the theme of a change of heart, promising that God would replace a stony heart with a heart of flesh (Ezekiel 11:19). Furthermore, he said God would give a new spirit within this new heart (Ezekiel 18:31-32). Within these two verses (31-32), may be found the basic doctrines of evangelistic preaching: (1) a righteous but forgiving God, (2) repentance, (3) regeneration, and (4) the work of the Holy Spirit within.

The New Testament doctrine of regeneration could not be preached more strikingly and with more hair-raising vividness than by a sermon based on Ezekiel's eerie description of the dry bones in the valley which received the breath of life from God (Ezekiel 37:1-10). Old-fashioned preaching? It is as old-fashioned as the preaching of these holy men of old.

Prophets Pressing the Invitation

Prophetic preaching is fervently evangelistic. The prophets concluded their sermons on the doctrines of grace with urgent invitations to people to repent, to trust God, to obey him, and to serve him. They made their appeals to the intellect, emotion, and will of a man. They appealed for decisions which were personal, imperative, final, and total commitment of life. Like Joshua, they challenged people; "Choose you this day whom you will serve" (Joshua 24:15).

The prophet Elijah on Mt. Carmel called in zealous urgency for a decision: "How long halt ye between two opinions? If the Lord be God, follow him: but if Baal, then follow him" (I Kings 1:18). When Elijah called fire down from heaven, he was what people today call a sensational evangelist.

Amos uttered stern warnings to Israel about the judgments that would come upon them inevitably, because of the wrath of God toward their sins. He exhorted, "Prepare to meet thy God!" (Amos 4:12). Amos was what modern people would call "a hell-fire and damnation" preacher.

The last chapter in Hosea's prophecy is a plea for a decision by his people to return to the Lord, the climax of a continual invitation to accept God's forgiving grace. He appeals, "Take with you words, and return unto the Lord; say unto him, Take away all iniquity, and receive us graciously." He was speaking like an evangelist giving an invitation at the close of his sermon. He was an emotional preacher.

Isaiah with his erudite mind called for a decision made by one's intellect and reasoning power, declaring that God is willing to help a sinner think through his problem of redemption. He invited, "Come now, and let us reason together, saith the Lord: though your sins be as scarlet, they shall be as white as snow; though they be red like crimson, they shall be as wool" (Isaiah 1:18). Isaiah was a scholarly evangelist, somewhat like a doctor of theology or a seminary teacher.

Ezekiel was one of Israel's most influential prophets. He was like a shepherding pastor to a flock of captive people. He alternated consolations and warnings, all the while interspersing gracious invitations and tender appeals. He urged them, "Cast away from you all your transgressions, whereby ye have transgressed: and make you a new heart and a new spirit, for why will ye die, O house of Israel?" (Ezekiel 18:31). Ezekiel was what people now would call a pastor-evangelist.

When Isaiah foresaw the Saviour so clearly and preached about him so winsomely (Isaiah 53), it is no wonder that he gave such a spiritual, heart-searching, and appealing evangelistic invitation: "Ho, every one that thirsteth, come ye to the waters, and he that hath no money; come ye, buy, and eat: yea, come, buy wine and milk without money and without price" (Isaiah 55:1). The prophet's mind was flashing like lightning, his heart was ablaze with love, and his tongue seems to have been touched with a live coal from off the altar of heaven. His invitation song had something of a "hallelujah chorus" in it. He was a Spirit-filled, Christ-centered evangelist.

When one preaches about the Christ of God, as this ancient prophet did, a yearning for the salvation of lost souls will burst out in a persuasive exhortation to accept God's offer of salvation. Isaiah earnestly wooed the people: "Seek ye the Lord while he may be found, call ye upon him while he is near: let the wicked forsake his way, and the unrighteous man his thoughts: and let him return unto the Lord" (Isaiah 55:6-7). A preacher with such a message about salvation through Christ, as Isaiah delivered, always seems to come on beautiful feet, beautiful indeed to those to whom he brings the good tidings of salvation and peace (Isaiah 52:7).

FOR BIBLE STUDY AND DISCUSSION

1. What is the Bible's justification for having evangelists? What are their Scriptural qualifications?
2. In what area of a man's life does sin begin? How did Jesus illustrate it in the Sermon on the Mount?
3. What is Scriptural repentance? What things may be confused with it but fall short?
4. In what right spirit and in what wrong spirit may a preacher denounce specific sins?
5. What should be included and made plain in an invitation to accept salvation through Christ?

CHAPTER NINE

PREPARING THE WAY OF THE LORD

> "The next day John seeth Jesus coming unto
> him, and saith, Behold, the Lamb of God,
> which taketh away the sin of the world."
>
> —John 1:29

The people of Jerusalem were milling around the streets in noisy excitement. "Have you heard about that sensational preacher down by the Jordan who is attracting such tremendous crowds to hear him?" Brother asked brother; neighbor spoke to neighbor; friend told friend. "Let us get on our donkeys and ride down to the Jordan to hear him. He is really getting people told about their sins," they said. The news was spreading like fire in the breeze.

John the Baptist had burst into the attention of all Judea. No prophet had been heard among the Jews since Malachi, about four hundred years before. The people knew that a genuine prophet had arisen. They knew by his likeness to Elijah whom they respected so highly, knew by the ring of sincerity in his voice, knew by the stinging directness with which he condemned sin, knew by the zeal and sense of urgency with which he appealed for repentance, knew by the widespread revival which he was leading so vigorously.

The people thought, "This man has come from God, this dynamic herald telling of the nearness of the Messianic kingdom for which our people have been looking for centuries." The complacent, dignified, proud old rulers at Jerusalem had been accustomed to people coming to them; this time they went out to see the fearless, dead-in-earnest preacher who sounded like he knew what he was talking about, and who believed what he was saying. He sounded like a man who had a message from God to proclaim to his generation. He was claiming that he was there to blaze out a royal highway for the Lord. People will go to hear a man like that, anytime.

Characteristics of the Prophet John

If John the Baptist is to be a criterion for young prophets today, they must differentiate between his mannerisms and his spiritual characteristics. John's camel-hair raiment and leather girdle would not be attractive in the First Church of a metropolitan area. Nor would wild honey and locust be on the menu in most places. Just so, it is not necessary to preach with such severity as John, nor to call people in church a brood of rattlesnakes! These were mannerisms in keeping with John's personality, which were assets to him but would be liabilities to other preachers. Prophets must be themselves, not mimics of the mannerisms of great men. When Billy Sunday was the most publicized evangelist in America, many "little Billys" all over the nation met their downfall by trying to mimic Sunday's acrobatic antics in the pulpit or the tongue-lashing tactics which he used on other preachers and deacons. Christ is the norm, the ideal—not some contempory great man.

Some phases of John's career cannot be duplicated, but their spiritual meaning can be interpreted and appropriated. For example, not many can be born of a priestly line like John. His father Zacharias was a priest and his mother Elizabeth was a descendant of Aaron. But a young prophet is blessed if he has a noble heritage from godly forbears, and if he was reared in a Christian home. Not every young prophet today can be reared among the silent solitudes of the mountains and prairies, like John was reared in the hill country of Judea. But every young prophet should take time to go alone with God for Bible study, meditation on the truth, prayer for the Spirit's guidance, and committal of himself to the will of the Father. Not every young preacher can have a towering personality like John. But every God-called young man can try to think like a prophet, to live like a prophet, to pray like a prophet, and to preach like a prophet.

Many of the spiritual characteristics of John the Baptist must be built into the character and conduct of a prophet if he comes into mature usefulness. A prophet of God must not be a worshipper of popularity, like a reed blown in every direction by the varying winds of current popular opinions (Matthew 11:7-10). Nor should one be a pink-tea prophet dressed in silks and satins, currying favor with the privileged classes (Matthew 11:8). He must have character.

John the Baptist was more than a prophet. He was a man of God who had a heaven-given commission to perform, and he was a man of action ready to do it. John was called of God to deliver a message about the Messiah who was coming immediately to establish the kingdom of heaven. Every effective prophet has some great essential message running through all his messages. It seems that John was never unconscious of what his divinely-imposed task in life was, never for one moment did he forget it. He had no church building in which to preach, but since he was under divine compulsion to preach he began to cry in the wilderness. He preached with fervor and passion and power about the King and the kingdom (Matthew 3:1-3).

An out-door preacher like John the Baptist must attract the attention of the passing throng to compel people to stop and listen. He also must hold their attention or they will walk off and leave him. He must speak in the language of ordinary people, and use it with such clarity that all can understand both his words and his theme. The spiritual characteristics of the preaching of John may be used as a measuring rod for the qualities needed by preachers today. His preaching "stabbed people awake" when they heard him. He used sharp-pointed words of one or two syllables. He employed vivid metaphors to illustrate his points. Fire! Judgment! Repent! Wrath is coming; flee! Offspring of snakes! Axe at the root of the trees! The threshing floor of God! Chaff to be burned! Unquenchable fire! The Messianic rule is at hand, as near as your right hand! Live right to prove that you have repented! Be baptized! "We never heard such preaching before," thought the people.

In spite of his popular appeal, John was to become an all-time criterion for preachers in his humility and self-effacement. He vigorously denied that he was the Messiah. When Jesus began to gain popular favor, John immortalized himself by his utter lack of ministerial jealousy—that perennial temptation of preachers. When people began to tell John that Jesus was growing more popular than he was, he made the classic answer, "He must increase, but I must decrease" (John 3:30).

In his preaching John had a sense of urgency born of the belief that he had a life-and-death message from God. He preached that message with unwavering moral conviction and death-defying courage. Most significantly, John was inflamed with the indwelling Holy Spirit. This gave him a contagious enthusiasm which drew people to hear him and persuaded them to believe him. A man can always get some followers if he himself believes deeply enough in what he is preaching. John was what someone has called a Jesus-intoxicated man.

John's Heritage from Other Prophets

John the Baptist was the last of the Old-Testament-type prophets; he opened the door of the new era under Christ. It was inevitable that he should inherit many characteristics and qualities from the prophets of former centuries. God grant that present-day prophets may do the same.

John felt an overpowering sense of mission to fulfill the prophecy of Isaiah (Isaiah 40:3-5), that is, to build a royal highway of spiritual truth over which the Messiah should enter his ministry to men. He was convinced that he was the one prophesied by Malachi when he said, "Behold, I will send my messenger, and he shall prepare the way before me" (Malachi 3:1), that he was the promised Elijah (Malachi 4:5). A Christian today becomes gloriously useful when he is spurred on to work diligently at some clearly-understood task, believing that he has a personal call of God to accomplish that task.

John's heritage from the older prophets was multiform. He was strikingly like Elijah in his ascetic life, his eccentric dress, his sudden appearance, his severe preaching, and his fearless denouncement of the sins of royal persons. He was like Amos in his unrestrained and uncompromising cry against the social sins of his time. He was like Isaiah in foreseeing the atoning work of the Lamb of God (Isaiah 53:6-7). He was like Jeremiah, Hosea, Ezekiel,

Jonah, and many others who preached unceasingly that the people must repent of sin. He was like Micah in his concern for people who were being defrauded or being treated violently. He was like Joel as he preached about the baptism of the Holy Ghost and of fire. He was like Zechariah who preached in plain, easily-understood, straight-from-the-shoulder, pointed language about ethics in daily living. He was more optimistic about the future than Zechariah, because the Messianic reign which Zechariah saw but dimly was "at hand" in John's time.

John's Message to Men, Then and Now

One of the persistent cries from the pew of today is for preaching that is relevant to the life of the listeners. Life is so full of vital questions and vexing problems; the Bible is full of applicable texts and revealing answers. John fitted the Old Testament Scriptures to every-day sins. No one ever accused John the Baptist of preaching "over the heads" of the congregation!

John's sermons had a vital doctrinal content, the kind of content without which no preaching can be truly great or permanently effective. He preached great doctrines such as the holiness of God, the sinfulness of sin, the inevitable judgment to come, the necessity for repentance, the call to obedience, the life of social righteousness, the glorious redemption through the Lamb of God, and the need for the baptism of the Holy Spirit.

John put refreshing fruit around the doctrinal core of his sermons by making practical applications to the lives of his hearers. He told those who were collecting taxes for the Roman government that they must be honest and fair to all. Today, he would tell men to tell the truth when making out their income tax returns. He admonished the soldiers to refrain from cruel violence. Today, he probably would talk about the crime wave, social injustice, or race prejudice. He demanded that rich people share their garments and wealth with the poor who had none. Today, probably he would talk about slum clearance, fair wages to share-croppers, education for needy children, and feeding the hungry in poverty-stricken lands. He exhorted all to be content with their paychecks. Today, he would preach about righteousness between management and labor, about violence in strikes, and against crass worship of money.

John poured pitiless scorn on the nationally proud Jews who thought they were automatically born children of God merely because they were descendants of Abraham, and that, therefore, they were free from the judgment to come.

This was vital preaching. John demanded character, a character that was revealed by righteousness, a righteousness that proved the reality of repentance. He called for immediate decisions, public confessions and professions of faith, and baptism as a symbol of what was experienced in their hearts.

All of this vital and pointed preaching by John the Baptist led up to the ultimate objective of all prophetic preaching then and now, that is, preaching Christ and pointing men to him. "Behold the Lamb of God!" cried the Baptist in excitement and exhilaration. This is the pinnacle of prophetic preaching. John seemed to be conscious that he had reached the climax of all Old Testament prophecy when he directed men to look at the Lamb of God, the Messiah, the desired of all nations and ages. The torch of Messianic hope had been held up by the prophets through the centuries, burning brighter and brighter as the years came and went. It was as bright as sunrise when John pointed to Jesus and gave an exultant shout. To the prophets of today it is a light as brilliant as the noonday sun in an unclouded sky.

FOR BIBLE STUDY AND DISCUSSION

1. What is the New Testament meaning of the kingdom of heaven, or the kingdom of God? Is there any difference between the two?
2. When John the Baptist was in prison why was he confused about who Jesus was (Matthew 11:3)?
3. What did Jesus mean (Matthew 3:11) about John being the greatest one ever born of woman, yet saying that the least in the kingdom of heaven would be greater than he?
   (See John A. Broadus, *An American Commentary on the New Testament,* Vol. I Philadelphia: American Baptist Publication Society, 1886. See A. T. Robertson, *Word Pictures in the New Testament,* Vol. I., Sunday School Board, Nashville, 1930).
4. Did John purposely imitate the many prophets from whom he had so rich a heritage?
5. Are there times when certain sermons do not justify or call for any references to Christ?
6. What in this study has impressed you most, and has blessed you most?